A Complete Guide for Celebrating Seven Holidays

HANDBOOK of BIBLE

Festivals

GALEN PETERSON

STANDARD PUBLISHING
Cincinnati, Ohio

Library of Congress Cataloging-in-Publication Data

Peterson, Galen
    Handbook of Bible festivals : a complete guide for
celebrating the holidays / Galen Peterson.
      p.   cm.
    Includes bibliographical references and index.
    ISBN 0-7847-0595-X
    1. Fasts and feasts in the Bible—Study and teaching. 2. Fasts
and feasts—Judaism—Study and teaching. I. Title.
BS1199.F35P48   1997
263' .97—dc20   96-41862
                                    CIP

© 1997 by The Standard Publishing Company, Cincinnati, Ohio
A division of Standex International Corporation
All rights reserved
Printed in the United States of America
04 03 02 01 00 99 98 97   5 4 3 2 1

Contents

*reproducible

The Festival Calendar

The calendar of biblical days was arranged according to twelve lunar months. Periodically a thirteenth "leap" month was added to bring the calendar in conformity to the solar year of 365 1/4 days. The holidays, also known as feasts, were associated with the seasons and had an agricultural character. Seven feasts were ordained by God in Leviticus 23. The first two—Passover and Unleavened Bread—have been blended into the single holiday of Passover, and First Fruits has become part of Pentecost. The establishment of Purim was later made in the book of Esther. Hanukkah does not have a scriptural injunction or basis but was set during the time between the writing of the Old and New Testaments and was an annual holiday in the days of Jesus.

Calendar of Biblical Festivals

Biblical month	Modern equivalent	Festival	Theme	O.T. Reference	N.T. Reference
Nisan	March/April	**Passover** (unleavened bread)	Redemption from slavery in Egypt, spiritual redemption	Exodus 12:1–51 Leviticus 23:5–8	Matthew 26:17–30 Mark 14:12–26 Luke 22:1–38 John 13:1–20
Iyar	April/May				
Sivan	May/June	**Pentecost** (First Fruits)	The giving of the Law and of the Holy Spirit	Exodus 19 Leviticus 23:15–21	Acts 2:1–47
Tammuz	June/July				
Av	July/August				
Elul	August/September				
Tishri	September/October	**Trumpets/ New Year** **Day of Atonement** **Tabernacles**	Use of trumpets, sacrifice Forgiveness Dwelling with God	Leviticus 23:23–35 Numbers 29:1–6 Leviticus 16:1–34; 23:26–28 Leviticus 23:33–36, 39–44	1 Thessalonians 4:16 Hebrews 9:11—10:22; 13:11, 12 John 7:2—9:5
Heshvan	October/November				
Kislev	November/December	**Hanukkah**	Miracles and servanthood		John 10:22, 23
Tevet	December/January				
Shevat	January/February				
Adar	February/March	**Purim**	God's preservation of Israel	Esther 9:23–32	

Introduction

You are about to set forth on an exciting adventure to rediscover the holidays of the Bible. This book is designed to include these meaningful, yet often overlooked, festivals in special programs. Each program can be completed in less than an hour and is well suited for use in Sunday school, club and summer day camp settings. Christian schools will find many opportunities for using these festivals during the school year.

These materials provide a hands-on learning experience that will enable us to understand the history behind each holiday. Key principles will unfold that will help us grow in our faith. We will see with our eyes, hear with our ears, do crafts with our hands, and even taste the various features of the festivals, giving us a lasting memory and a better understanding of the Bible.

How is the Lord's Supper actually observed during a Passover? Why were trumpets blown on the Feast of Trumpets? What did it mean to dwell in temporary shelters during the Feast of Tabernacles? What's a grogger? The answers to these questions and many more can be found in the pages to follow.

And leaders need not be afraid of venturing into the Jewish culture! There are easy-to-use guidelines, lists of materials needed, recipes that tell how to prepare traditional foods, and suggestions for leading the programs.

The holidays are arranged in the order in which they occur on the calendar, but they can be celebrated at any time. For each holiday, biblical and traditional customs are described. Their symbolism, fulfillment in Jesus, and modern-day applications are suggested.

Our God is the Master Designer of a plan for all people which he has creatively revealed in the festival days. Let us join together in a unique journey back in time and into a world where God has interwoven his message of redemption. And, as we shall discover, it is a place with room for young and old alike. It offers experiences from yesteryear with applications for today.

Now, let the adventure begin . . .

The Feast  of Passover

Pesach

BIBLICAL MONTH	*Nisan*
MODERN EQUIVALENT	March/April
O.T. REFERENCE	Exodus 12:1-51; Leviticus 23:5-8
N.T. REFERENCE	Matthew 26:17-30; Mark 14:12-26
	Luke 22:1-38; John 13:1-20

An Overview

Passover is traditionally celebrated as a *seder* (SAY-der)—a specific order of events contained in a text called a *Haggadah* (hah-gah-DAH), meaning "the telling." In this celebration, a specially designed *Haggadah* will allow participants to tell the Passover story and eat the ceremonial foods. They can also sing an easy-to-learn Passover folk song called *"Dayeinu"* (dah-YEY-noo). Through this observance, they will be able to understand the historical basis of Passover as well as the symbolic meaning that is fulfilled in the true Lamb of God—Jesus the Messiah.

Biblical Heritage

As told in the first twelve chapters of Exodus, the original observance of Passover took place on the eve of the release of the Israelites from slavery in Egypt, about 1500 years B.C. Ten plagues were brought upon the Egyptians to cause Pharaoh to free the Israelites, culminating with the plague that brought death to the firstborn in the land. But God provided a way for the Israelites to escape this plague. Each household was to take a lamb that had no flaws, slay it, and place its blood on the doorway of the home. The people were also told by God to eat the lamb, together with *matzah* (MAHT-sah, meaning "unleavened bread" without any yeast that causes bread to rise), and bitter herbs. The Israelites were, in fact, "passed over" on that night of the plague of death and were set free the following day. Then began the forty years of wandering in the Sinai wilderness.

Historical Observance

While in the wilderness, Passover became an annual commemoration for the Jewish people (Exodus 12:14). A second feast, called Unleavened Bread, also began during this time (Exodus 12:15; Leviticus 23:6-8). Leavening in Scripture is symbolic of sin (Leviticus 6:17; Hosea 7:4). According to God's instructions, the people were to eat unleavened bread for seven days after Passover. Later, when the temple was established in Jerusalem, Passover and Unleavened Bread merged into one holiday. It also became one of three pilgrimage feasts. (Pentecost and Tabernacles were the other two.)

When the people arrived in Jerusalem on their pilgrimage to the feast, they would purchase lambs. Then, during the afternoon before the observance of Passover, the heads of households would bring the lambs to the temple courtyard. There, in the presence of priests, they would slay their lambs and then return to their homes or the place where they were staying temporarily. After sundown, large families (or mixed groups of individuals and small families) would gather together for the Passover celebration. As the people reclined on cushions around the room, they drank a glass of wine and ate the meal of lamb, unleavened bread and bitter herbs. It was the custom to dip the bitter herbs in saltwater to remember the bitterness of slavery in Egypt. Another symbolic ritual involved the *afikomen matzah* (ah-fee-KO-men MAHT-sah), which represented the coming Messiah. This ceremony also included telling the original Passover story with the children asking questions. Three additional cups of wine were used and the *Hallel* (ha-LELL, Psalms 113–118) was sung.

Modern Observance

The celebration of Passover today is very similar to that of the ancient way, with one notable exception—no longer is a sacrificed lamb the central feature of the holiday. Unleavened bread has actually become the principal element of the festival. Orthodox families thoroughly clean their homes just before Passover and all crumbs with *chometz* (hah-METS, meaning "leavening") are collected and burned. Some families also use separate dishes that have never touched leavened food on Passover .

The ceremony itself has become organized in a set order called a *seder*. The service is read from a book known as the *Haggadah*. It contains the liturgy, instructions for eating the ceremonial food, readings from the original Passover story, songs, and prayers. Since Talmudic times, it has been customary to set a place at the table for Elijah the prophet who was said to be the forerunner of the Messiah. (The Talmud is a rabbinical commentary that was compiled in Babylon and Jerusalem during the second to fifth centuries A.D.) A cup of wine is set out for Elijah and a door opened in anticipation of his arrival. Children search for the hidden *afikomen matzah* and when they find it the leader redeems it. (The children receive money or candy as a ransom.) The rabbinical interpretation of the *afikomen* is that its origin is unknown and that it represents dessert or the end of entertainment.

Changes in Observance

In spite of the retention of much of the biblical character of Passover, the modern observance has lost much of its Messianic symbolism. With the destruction of the temple in Jerusalem in A.D. 70, it was no longer possible to slaughter the lambs under priestly supervision. Thus the feature of the lamb was discarded, resulting in the minimizing of the rich symbolism of the Passover lamb that was without spot or blemish, slain in innocence, and whose blood was placed on the doors of the Israelite homes to spare them from the plague of death. The symbol of the *afikomen* also lost its original meaning. It is a Greek word meaning "I came" and was probably given the meaning "The Coming One" in second temple times. It is likely that either the confusion resulting from the dispersion of Israel after A. D. 70 or rabbinical reinterpretation of the word led to its different meaning today. However, the *afikomen,* together with the third cup of Passover wine which immediately followed this piece of unleavened bread, was used by Jesus to confirm his impending death as the Messianic Lamb of God (Isaiah 53), and at the same time became the bread and the cup of the Lord's Supper.

How can we reconcile the seeming paradox of Jesus and his disciples keeping the Passover together before the actual day of observance? The answer lies in the way that the Passover was kept by many Jews after the building of the temple. Originally, while Israel wandered in the wilderness, they kept the Passover on the fourteenth of *Nisan*. But later in the Pentateuch, a door was opened for a shift in the observance. According to Deuteronomy 16:6, once the temple was built in Jerusalem, Passover could be celebrated on the anniversary of the departure from Egypt, which was on the fifteenth of *Nisan* (Numbers 33:3). Consequently, in Jesus' day, some people were keeping the Passover on the fourteenth and others on the fifteenth of *Nisan*, thus allowing him to observe the feast with his disciples and then to be crucified at the very moment when the Passover lambs were being slain for the observance by the majority of the people (Matthew 27:45; Babylonian Talmud, *Mishnah Pesahim* 58a).

The Passover holds great meaning for our lives today. It is a commemoration of the sparing of the Israelites from the plague of death and slavery in Egypt, as well as the sparing of believers in Jesus the Messiah from the plague of eternal death and slavery to sin.

Application

When the reading of the *Haggadah* is completed, talk about the meaning of Passover. Begin by discussing the concept of leavening.
What does the leavening do to dough? (It causes it to rise when yeast or baking powder is added.) How is it like sin? (It spreads throughout our lives when we let it get started. For example, when we tell a lie, it becomes easier to steal something.) The Bible teaches that God wants us to stop sinning.

> *"Get rid of the old yeast that you may be a new batch without yeast—as you really are. For Christ, our Passover Lamb, has been sacrificed" (1 Corinthians 5:7).*

Review the concept of "passing over" our sins.
What happened to the homes of the Egyptians who did not have the blood of the Passover Lamb on their doors? (Their firstborn sons died.) What sign did the blood on the doorways make? (a cross) Jesus became the perfect Passover Lamb. When we believe in him, what will God do about our sins? (He will pass over them and forgive us.) The Scriptures say that we can be like Moses:

> *"By faith he kept the Passover and the sprinkling of blood, so that the destroyer of the firstborn would not touch the firstborn of Israel" (Hebrews 11:28).*

Trace the beginning of the Lord's Supper.
When did the Lord's Supper begin? (It began during the last Passover celebrated by Jesus and his disciples.) By keeping the Lord's Supper, we are being obedient to Jesus' instructions. Matthew writes about this kind of obedience.

> *"So the disciples did as Jesus had directed them and prepared the Passover"*
> *(Matthew 26:19).*

Preparation

Read Leviticus 23:5-8; Exodus 12.

Make sufficient copies of the *Haggadah* (pages 13-23) for all participants.

A *Haggadah* provides the complete narrative and instructions for a presentation of Passover. The leader performs the various ceremonies of Passover and says the traditional blessings (in transliterated Hebrew and English). The participants take turns reading brief portions of the *Haggadah.* Alternatively, adults can read all parts of the text while younger children listen and participate in the "hands-on" portion of the program.

Learn the tune to the song *"Dayeinu."* See page 24.

Obtain the following foods and supplies:
- ❏ **Elijah's chair**—an empty chair at a table
- ❏ **Elijah's cup**—a decorative goblet (a regular glass will suffice) on the table next to the empty chair
- ❏ **Grape juice**—enough for each child to have four drinks (sips)
- ❏ **Cups**—the cups are filled during the program
- ❏ **Matzah**—Wrap three whole portions of *matzah* in a napkin. Matzot (maht-ZOAT, the plural form of the word) come in boxes of 12-15. The extra *matzot* will be needed if the group is large but can be kept in the box until required.
- ❏ **A bowl of saltwater** for dipping parsley
- ❏ **Rewards**—candy or coins for the finder of the hidden matzah
- ❏ **A seder plate** (a plate that has designated places for the food). A large regular plate can easily be substituted.

Place the following items on the seder plate:

- ☐ **A bone** (Ideally a lamb shank bone but a turkey drumstick will suffice.)
- ☐ Sprigs of **parsley**
- ☐ A scoop of **horseradish**
- ☐ A scoop of *haroset* (hah-RO-set)—mixture of applesauce, raisins, and almonds or walnuts

Arrange for room set-up and helpers.

If the group is small, sit together around one table. Larger groups can sit in a big circle with a view of a table where the leader stands.

It is helpful if adults can assist children in distributing and preparing the foods.

With larger groups, save time by using pitchers of juice and *seder* plates on several tables.

Decide how to present the application of the celebration to contemporary living.

The Celebration

Read the *Haggadah*.

The instructions for this celebration of Passover are included in the *Haggadah* on the following pages. This version blends traditional elements with their Messianic symbolism and fulfillment. Those portions that are not found in a traditional *Haggadah* are *italicized* for easy identification. (Hebrew and Yiddish terms are italicized throughout this book.)

A Passover *Haggadah*

Leader

The holiday of Passover is celebrated each year in the spring. The instructions for observing this holiday are found in the *Haggadah,* a Hebrew word meaning, 'the telling.' This book tells the story of the first Passover when the nation of Israel was freed from slavery in Egypt long ago. The celebration is called a *seder.* It follows a special order of events, beginning with the first of four toasts.

The Cup of Sanctification

Cups are filled with fruit of the vine, grape juice.

Leader

Let us lift our cups together as I say the Hebrew blessing which is said before all holiday meals.

"Ba-RUKE a-TAH ah-doe-NI el-o-HEY-nu MEL-eck ha-o-LAM BO-ray pree ha-GAFF-en."

"Blessed are you, O Lord our God, King of the Universe, who creates the fruit of the vine."

© 1997

"Blessed are you, O Lord our God, King of the Universe, who gives us life and allows us to enjoy this festive holiday."

All people drink the first cup.

Karpas

Each person takes a piece of parsley called karpas (CAR-pahs).

Leader

We now dip our parsley in saltwater. Saltwater is like tears from crying. It reminds us of the tears shed by the people of Israel when they were slaves in Egypt.

All dip parsley in saltwater.

Leader

Hold your parsley as I say the blessing.

"Ba-RUKE a-TAH ah-doe-NI el-o-HEY-nu MEL-eck ha-o-LAM BO-ray pree ha-ah-doh-MAH."

"Blessed are you, O Lord our God, King of the Universe, who creates the fruit of the earth."

The parsley is eaten.

Breaking the *Matzah*

The leader takes the middle *matzah* from the set of three and breaks it in half, leaving one part, and places the second part in a napkin.

Holding this *matzah,* the leader explains

Matzah is the Hebrew word for unleavened bread. This one special piece of *matzah* is called the *afikomen* (ah-fee-KO-men), a word that means 'I came.' *Many people do not realize this when they celebrate Passover, but the matzah is a reference to Jesus the Messiah who came in fulfillment of prophecy.*

The *afikomen* is hidden by the leader, to be found later.

The leader takes the remaining *matzah* and says

Behold, this is the poor bread which our ancestors ate in the land of Egypt. Let anyone who is hungry come in and eat; let anyone who is needy come in and celebrate Passover.

The Four Questions

The Youngest Reader

Why is this day different from all

other days? On other days we eat leavened bread; on this day we eat only *matzah.* On other days we eat all kinds of herbs; on this day we eat only bitter herbs. On other days we do not dip herbs at all; on this day we dip them twice. On other days we eat in an ordinary manner; on this day we eat in a celebration.

Leader

To find the answer to these questions we must go back to the early history of Israel, to the days of Moses and Aaron, and recall the story as if we were there ourselves. We are to imagine ourselves as the slaves of Pharaoh in Egypt, and how the Lord our God took us out from there.

The Four Sons

Leader

According to tradition, four sons have questions about Passover. The first son is the wise son. He asks:

Another Reader

What is the meaning of all these laws that we have been commanded in the Holy Scriptures? Why are they important?

Leader

He is very interested in understanding why we observe this holiday. He wants to follow God's laws and to understand their importance. We answer him by teaching him all the things that the Lord has given us to understand about the Passover *and the way that Passover points the way to the Messiah.*

The second son is the foolish son. How does he word his question?

Another Reader

What is the purpose of this Passover service which God commanded you?

Leader

"You" he says, and not "us." His way of asking the question shows that he wants to act on his own, even without God in his life. We answer him by quoting the verse: "It is because of that which the Lord did for me when I came forth from Egypt." The Exodus from Egypt was a personal victory for every person. Feeling the way he does, there is no doubt the foolish son would have stayed behind in slavery in Egypt *and today would not want to receive the salvation offered by the Messiah.*

The third son is the simple son. How does he ask his question about Passover?

Another Reader

What is this?

Leader

These things are so important that they confuse him. Such a son requires a clear answer that will impress him immediately: The Passover proves the power of God who brought us out of the land of Egypt and also gives us eternal life.

The fourth son does not know how to ask a question. He needs help in answering the question that is surely in his mind, but he doesn't seem able to ask. We say to him: "This holiday of freedom is being celebrated by each of us because of those things the Lord has done for me. He has called me to come forth from Egypt, *and he has called me to live with him forever by believing in Jesus the Messiah."*

The Story of Passover

Another Reader

In early times, a man named Abraham began a family that traveled to the land of Egypt. While they were there, they grew into a nation called Israel.

Another Reader

But all the people became slaves of Pharaoh, the king of Egypt. The Israelites worked long hours in the fields and built the great cities of the Pharaohs.

Another Reader

The people of Israel cried to God for their rescue. God heard their prayers and so he called Moses to lead and help them. God said to Moses from a burning bush: "I will send you to Pharaoh, and you shall say, the Lord God of Israel has commanded: 'Let my people go.'"

Another Reader

Moses went to Pharaoh and asked for the freedom of the Israelites. But Pharaoh refused to listen, saying: "Who is the Lord that I should obey his voice? I do not know the Lord. And I will not let Israel go."

The Ten Plagues
(Assign the plagues to various readers.)

Leader

Because Pharaoh refused to listen, horrible plagues were sent upon Egypt.

Blood

All the waters of Egypt, the rivers, streams, and ponds were turned into blood.

Frogs

And Aaron, the brother of Moses, stretched out his hand over the waters of Egypt and frogs came up and covered the land.

Lice

Then Aaron stretched out his hand and the dust of the earth turned into lice throughout all the land of Egypt. Lice were upon man and upon beast.

Swarms of Flies

And there came a great swarm of flies upon the house of Pharaoh and in all the land of Egypt.

Cattle Plague

And Pharaoh still would not listen. Then there came a great plague upon all the cattle and other animals in Egypt.

Boils

And because of the hardness of Pharaoh's heart, boils broke out on the skin of all the people of Egypt.

Hail

Moses stretched out his rod and the Lord sent lightning and hail upon the land of Egypt, destroying their crops and trees.

Locusts

And an east wind brought locusts, eating everything that the hail had left. And not one green thing could be seen in the land of Egypt.

Darkness

And Moses stretched forth his rod toward heaven, and there was deep darkness in all the land of Egypt for three days.

Slaying of the firstborn

And it came to pass at midnight, the firstborn sons in the land of Egypt died. And there was a great cry in Egypt, for there was death in every Egyptian home.

Another Reader

But the sons of Israel were spared.

The Lord had commanded every family to take a lamb that had nothing wrong with it and sacrifice it in the evening.

Another Reader

God said: "Take the blood and put it on the two sides and on the top of the doors of your houses. Roast the lamb and eat it with unleavened bread and bitter herbs. This is the Lord's Passover."

Another Reader

"For I will pass through the land of Egypt this night and all the firstborn in the land of Egypt will die. But when I see the blood, I will pass over you and you will be spared."

Leader

Only in the houses where God's instructions for salvation had been followed, by placing the blood of the lamb upon their doorposts, did the Lord pass over in judgment.

This is also a picture of what happened later to Jesus, who was called the Lamb of God. So today, only those people who have been symbolically covered by the blood of Jesus and have followed God's instructions for salvation will be "passed over" in final judgment.

Another Reader

Pharaoh said to Moses: "Go forth from Egypt, both you and the children of Israel. Go and serve the Lord, as you have said."

Leader

So, our God took us from Egypt; he brought judgment upon our enemies; he allowed us to pass through the Red Sea; he met our needs in the wilderness; he gave us the Scriptures; *he sent us our Savior.* May we thank him and praise his name!

Everyone

For all God's blessings we are grateful. Blessed is his name.

Dayeinu

Leader

Now we are going to sing a traditional Passover song called *"Dayeinu"* ("We Would Have Been Grateful")

1. If the Lord, the Lord had rescued,
   Only rescued us from Egypt,
   Just the rescue would have been
   enough for us.
Chorus: Da-da-yei-nu, da-da-yei-nu, da-da-yei-nu, da-yei-nu, da-yei-nu, da-yei-nu. Da-da-yei-nu, da-da-yei-nu, da-da-yei-nu, da-yei-nu, da-yei-nu.

2. If the Lord, the Lord had given,
Only given us the Sabbath,
Just the Sabbath would have been
enough for us.

Chorus

3. If the Lord, the Lord had given,
Only given us the Torah,
Just the Torah would have been
enough for us.

Chorus

Holding the shank bone, the leader continues.

Concerning the Passover lamb, we have today only a shank bone as part of our observance. It is a reminder of how the blood sacrifice of the original Passover lamb spared the people from the plague of death.

Moses said to Israel, "Slay the Passover lamb and take a bunch of hyssop (a flowering plant) and dip it in the blood which is in the basin and apply some of the blood to the top and to the two sides of the door."

This action, by its very motions from the basin to the top of the door and across from side to side, was a picture of the cross where, many years later, the true Lamb of God, Jesus, would shed his blood. Because of his final and complete sacrifice, we can be spared from the plague of eternal death.

Another Reader

The Lord our God has given us his Word so that we may understand these truths.

The Bible says about Jesus: "Worthy is the Lamb that has been slain, to receive power, and riches, and wisdom, and might, and honor, and glory, and blessing."

Holding the *matzah*, the leader continues.

This unleavened bread, why do we eat it? Leaven makes bread rise and become soft and airy. Just a little bit of leaven will make a whole loaf of bread rise.

Since there was not enough time for the dough of our ancestors to leaven before the Lord freed them from Egypt, he commanded them to eat unleavened bread.

The Bible tells us that leaven is like sin. When we do one thing that is disobedient to God, our whole lives can become that way.

Even though God forgives us when we sin, this unleavened bread is a reminder that we must try to live our lives in a way that is faithful to God.

Holding the bitter herb, the leader continues.

These bitter herbs, what is the reason for them? It is because the lives of our ancestors were made bitter in the land of Egypt through hard service. We remember their sorrows, *but we are grateful that God has delivered us from spiritual sorrow through the Sacrificed Lamb.* We must also care for other people today, whose lives are filled with bitterness.

Another Reader

Let all of us think and act as if we had been rescued from Egypt. God has brought us from slavery to freedom from sin and from sorrow to joy.

Everyone

Therefore we praise, thank, glorify and adore God who performed all these miracles for our ancestors and for us.

The Cup of Deliverance

Leader

"Blessed are you, O Lord our God, King of the Universe, who redeemed us and our ancestors from Egypt, and has brought us to this night. So, O Lord our God, bring us to other festivals in coming days. Then shall we give thanks to you. Blessed are you, O Lord, Redeemer of Israel."

We now say the blessing over the second cup of Passover.

"Ba-RUKE a-TAH ah-doe-NI el-o-HEY-nu MEL-eck ha-o-LAM BO-ray pree ha-GAFF-en."

"Blessed are you, O Lord our God, King of the Universe, who creates the fruit of the vine."

The second cup is drunk.

Matzah: Unleavened Bread

The leader takes the top *matzah*, breaks it, and gives a piece to each person. After distributing the *matzah*, the leader says the blessing.

"Ba-RUKE a-TAH ah-doe-NI el-o-HEY-nu MEL-eck ha-o-LAM ah-SHAIR kid-SHAH-noo bih MITS-vo-tahv vit-zee-VAH-noo all ah- kee-LAT MAHT-sah."

"Blessed are you, O Lord our God, King of the Universe, who has sanctified us by his commandments, and has commanded us to eat unleavened bread."

Bitter Herbs

Leader

According to tradition, a bit of maror (mah-ROAR), horseradish, is placed on the *matzah*. This is the second dipping of Passover.

After preparing the *matzah*, the leader says the blessing.

"Ba-RUKE a-TAH ah-doe-NI el-o-HEY-nu MEL-eck ha-o-LAM ah-SHAIR kid-SHAH-noo bih MITS-vo-tahv vit-zee-VAH-noo all ah-kee-LAT mah-ROAR."

"Blessed are you, O Lord our God, King of the Universe, who has sanctified us by his commandments and commanded us to eat bitter herbs."

Leader

And according to tradition, *haroset* (a mixture of apples, raisins and nuts) is added to the *matzah* and bitter herbs. You may eat the *matzah* sandwich whenever you have it prepared.

All taste the *matzah* "sandwich."

The Hidden Matzah

Children can search for the *afikomen matzah*. When it is found, the one who finds it "barters" with the leader for its return. After a price (candy, coins, etc.) for redemption is agreed upon, the leader reclaims the *matzah*.

Holding the *afikomen*, the leader says

The afikomen matzah, whose mysterious name means, "I came," is a symbol of the Messiah. Just as it is baked without leaven, Jesus was without sin. It has piercings and he was pierced on the cross. It has stripes from baking. By Messiah's wounds, our sins are forgiven. Just as it is broken, he was broken and died for us. And like the price that was paid to bring the afikomen back, Jesus paid the price for our salvation.

Leader

It was this afikomen matzah that Jesus used for what is now called the Lord's Supper or Communion. As it is written: "Jesus took unleavened bread, and when He had given thanks, He broke it saying, this is My body, which is given for you—

this do in remembrance of Me—I am the living bread which came down from heaven; if anyone eats of this bread, he shall live eternally. This bread is my flesh which I shall give for the life of the world."

Everyone takes a portion of the *afikomen* and eats the *matzah*.

The Cup of Redemption

Holding the cup, the leader says the blessing.

"Ba-RUKE a-TAH ah-doe-NI el-o-HEY-nu MEL-eck ha-o-LAM BO-ray pree ha-GAFF-en."

"Blessed are you, O Lord our God, King of the Universe, who creates the fruit of the vine."

Leader

This third cup of Passover was used by Jesus for the Lord's Supper or Communion. As it is also written: "And He took the cup and gave thanks, and gave it to them, saying, Drink from it, all of you, for this is My blood of the covenant, which is poured out for many for forgiveness of sins."

The third cup is drunk.

Leader

This part of the Passover service, which we call the "The Lord's Supper," we keep in remembrance of his sacrifice for us. Jesus the Messiah became our Passover Lamb, symbolized here by the unleavened bread and the fruit of the vine. Blessed is the Lord our God!

Hallel

Leader

According to the Scriptures, after the Lord's Supper, Jesus and his disciples sang the words from the Hallel (ha-LELL) —the Psalms of Praise. Let us praise him together.

Everyone

"Hallelujah! Praise O servants of the Lord.
Praise the name of the Lord.
Blessed be the Name of the Lord from this time forth and forever."

The Cup and Chair of Elijah

Lifting the cup of Elijah, the leader continues.

The Scriptures also tell us that a prophet like Elijah was to come and announce the arrival of the Messiah.

Traditionally, this cup of expectation, an empty chair, and an open door have represented Elijah's arrival. *But this type of prophet has already come, for it is written about John the Baptist: "This is the one that was spoken of by Isaiah the Prophet, saying, 'The voice of one crying in the wilderness, make ready the way of the Lord.'"*

A child is sent to the door and the leader continues.

So today, as we open the door, *it is not to invite the prophet to enter, but rather it represents our hearts which we open to the Lord our God, where he might enter and live with us. As it is written: "Behold, I stand at the door and knock; if anyone hears my voice and opens the door, I will come in to him, and will dine with him and he with me." Moreover, we have been promised that Messiah will come again, and we look forward to that day.*

The Cup of Acceptance

The leader says the blessing over the fourth cup of Passover.

"Ba-RUKE a-TAH ah-doe-NI el-o-HEY-nu MEL-eck ha-o-LAM BO-ray pree ha-GAFF-en."

"Blessed are you, O Lord our God, King of the Universe, who creates the fruit of the vine."

The fourth cup is drunk.

Leader

"May the Lord rule over us forever. May the Lord be blessed in Heaven and in earth. May the Lord sustain us and send us his blessings. *May the Lord allow us to see the day of Messiah's return.* May he who makes peace in his highest heavens grant peace to us and to all people. Amen."

May we also pray for the peace of Jerusalem as he has commanded. And, we say with the people of Israel, "Next year in Jerusalem!"

The leader ends with this prayer.

"O give thanks unto the Lord, for he is good. His mercy endures forever. Blessed is he that comes in the name of the Lord, and is faithful to God and seeks him with his whole heart. O give thanks unto the Lord, for he is good, for his mercy endures forever and ever. Amen."

Present the application of this celebration. See page 10.

Dayeinu

(We Would Have Been Grateful)

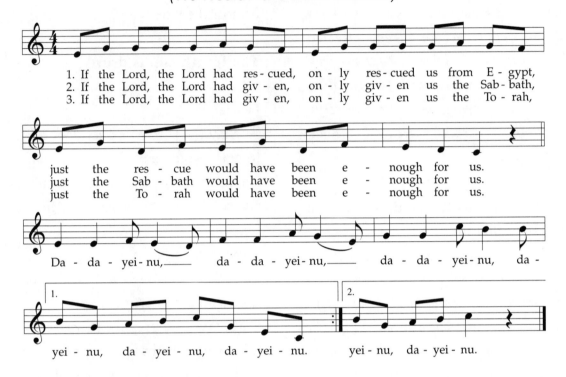

1. If the Lord, the Lord had res - cued, on - ly res - cued us from E - gypt,
2. If the Lord, the Lord had giv - en, on - ly giv - en us the Sab - bath,
3. If the Lord, the Lord had giv - en, on - ly giv - en us the To - rah,

just the res - cue would have been e - nough for us.
just the Sab - bath would have been e - nough for us.
just the To - rah would have been e - nough for us.

Da - da - yei - nu,___ da - da - yei - nu,___ da - da - yei - nu, da -

1. yei - nu, da - yei - nu, da - yei - nu.

2. yei - nu, da - yei - nu.

You're Invited

THE FEAST OF PASSOVER

Date

Time

Place

Please Come

The Feast

of

Pentecost

Shavuot (Weeks)

BIBLICAL MONTH	*Sivan*
MODERN EQUIVALENT	May/June
O.T. REFERENCE	Exodus 19; Leviticus 23:15-21
N.T. REFERENCE	Acts 2:1-47

An Overview

The Hebrew name for this holiday is *Shavuot* (shah-voo-OAT), meaning "weeks," because it is celebrated seven weeks plus one day after Passover. The Greek and English equivalent, Pentecost, takes its name from the number of days—50. Pentecost has two traditional themes. One is the *Torah* (TOE-rah) since it is believed that God gave the *Torah* to Moses on this day. The second is the harvest, since it comes at the time of the beginning of the grain harvest. We also know that the Holy Spirit came upon believers in a mighty way on this day. This celebration shows the remarkable connection between these three themes by telling the condensed stories of Moses on Mt. Sinai, Ruth, and the coming of the Holy Spirit in the book of Acts. A *Torah* scroll craft and one of several traditional cheese pastries round out the celebration.

Biblical Heritage

The word *Torah* is commonly translated "Law" but literally means "instruction" (from the root "to cast forth"). A careful study of Exodus 19 reveals that fifty days after the first Passover in Egypt, God gave Israel the *Torah* on Mt. Sinai. This event is prefaced in Exodus 19:1 with the words, "In the third month (*Sivan*) after the Israelites left Egypt, on the very day (meaning the first day of the month), they came to the desert of Sinai." Accounting for the sequence of events described in the verses that follow, Moses would have received the Law on the sixth of *Sivan*—fifty days after Passover. The Law was God's plan for living for the people of Israel. It set very high standards for holiness, worship and justice—standards which would prove to be very difficult for the people to keep without fault or omission.

Historical Observance

Leviticus 23 actually specifies two holy days associated with the Feast of Weeks. The first day, called "Firstfruits," was held on the day after the Sabbath (Leviticus 23:11). There has long been a debate over which Sabbath is cited here. Is it the weekly Sabbath or is it the special Sabbath of Unleavened Bread? The Sadducees, representing the conservative priests, interpreted the day of Firstfruits as the Sunday following Passover. The Pharisees, whose interpretations changed with the trends of the day, said it was the day after Unleavened Bread. In any event, on this day there was a simple ceremony. It involved presenting the first sheaf of the barley harvest before the Lord in the temple. There was to be no bread from the new grain eaten until the firstfruits sheaf had been dedicated to the Lord. It was a declaration of thankfulness to God by offering the first and finest part of the harvest.

The Hebrew word for "sheaf" is *omer* (OH-mare). This word has taken on a deeper meaning than just a cutting of grain. It is associated with the period of time following Firstfruits. The people were to count fifty days from the day of Firstfruits until the next sacred assembly in Jerusalem (Leviticus 23:15-21). On that return pilgrimage for the fiftieth day of the Feast of Weeks, they were to present two wave-loaves of bread made from wheat together with various burnt offerings. Other choice foods were brought along to Jerusalem as well.

According to the ancient rabbinical commentary *Mishnah*:

> When a man goes down to his field and sees for the first time a ripe fig or a ripe cluster of grapes or a ripe pomegranate, he binds it around with reed grass and says, "These are the firstfruits" (*Bikkurim 3:1*).

Modern Observance

Unlike other feasts which have been rabbinically modified, the first part of the Feast of Weeks—the day of Firstfruits—has been virtually ignored and is not observed today. The only related feature that has been retained is the beginning of the counting of the *omer* two days after Passover (following the practice of the ancient Pharisees). During this period a counting benediction is said daily:

"Blessed art Thou, O Lord our God, King of the universe, who has sanctified us by thy commandments, and has commanded us concerning the counting of the *Omer*. This is the ____ day, being ____ weeks and ____ days of the *Omer*."

Each day is updated until fifty days have been counted. Then on the fiftieth day, synagogue services are held commemorating the giving of the Law. On this night, many Orthodox Jews stay up all night reading the *Torah*. Also during these services, the book of Ruth is read. This tradition is based on a variety of reasons. First, in keeping with this holiday, Ruth is a story with a harvest theme. Second, Ruth was an ancestor of David and it is said that David was born and died on Pentecost. And third, because Ruth became a believer in the God of Israel, she would have accepted the precepts of the *Torah*.

Changes in Observance

We might ask the question, "Why isn't the first part of the Feast of Weeks observed by the Jewish community today?" Most rabbinical sources give no reason. But it is likely de-emphasized because of its association with the resurrection of Jesus. For on this very day, Jesus was resurrected from the dead. He was crucified on the eve of Passover, was in the tomb on the days of Passover and Unleavened Bread, and on the next day "Christ has been raised from the dead, the firstfruits of those who are asleep" (1 Corinthians 15:20).

In the Jewish culture, the last day of the Feast of Weeks is observed but in a significantly different manner from that of biblical times. Without a temple in Jerusalem there can be no sacrifices, and in a society no longer based on agriculture, the harvest theme is diminished. Thus the *Torah,* which was once related to this feast only in a secondary manner, has been elevated to a place of prominence. However, a very important factor has been overlooked in this change—the Law was difficult to comprehend and impossible to observe in perfection. So God foretold in Jeremiah and Ezekiel that he would one day write his Law on the hearts of his people (Jeremiah 31:33; Ezekiel 36:26). This would be accomplished through the coming of the Holy Spirit in a way that was unlike any other event in history.

In the days of the Old Testament, the Spirit was not universally and continually present with mankind. He moved in and out of circumstances on earth. He singularly inspired the prophets and other writers of Scripture. We see isolated incidents where he came upon people and empowered them. And, as in the cases of Samson and Saul, he also departed individuals. But this changed dramatically on one very special day of Pentecost fifty days after the death of Jesus (Acts 2). The Holy Spirit came to bring us comfort, to empower us for service, and to teach us God's truths. He came to convict the hearts of all people concerning sin. Only the Spirit of God enables us to live with his principles written on our hearts, becoming part of our personal identities. This is the connection between the giving of the Law and the coming of the Holy Spirit, both on the day of Pentecost.

What about the harvest theme of Pentecost as illustrated in the reading of the book of Ruth? Just as Ruth was part of a spiritual harvest by believing in the God of Israel, a greater harvest took place on that special day of Pentecost cited in Acts. It was a day when the household of faith would spread beyond the nation of Israel, bringing in a harvest of many peoples.

Leviticus 23:17 tells us that the people were required to bring two loaves of bread and to wave them as an offering of firstfruits to the Lord. One way of looking at this practice is that the two loaves are a symbol of Jew and Gentile, side by side, presented before the Lord and welcomed into his everlasting kingdom. Indeed the context of Acts 2 reveals that beginning on that day of Pentecost, the believing community of Israel became the "called out ones" (Greek, *ekklesia)* and began to include great numbers of people from many nations.

Application

After discussing the Old and New Testament stories, review the giving of the *Torah.*

What happened on that first day of Pentecost at Mt. Sinai? (God gave the Law to Moses.) Why did God give the Israelites the 613 commandments? (Commandments reveal standards for daily living, worship, God's holiness and humanity's sin, and requirements for having a relationship with God.) So the *Torah,* meaning the Law, is an important part of the Bible. In fact the Apostle Paul said about the Bible

"All Scripture is God-breathed and is useful for teaching, rebuking, correcting and training in righteousness" (2 Timothy 3:16).

We should read the Bible so that we can understand the ways of God.

Examine the sending of the Holy Spirit.

Later on the day of Pentecost as noted in the book of Acts, God did something else to help us understand the ways of God. What was it? (He sent the Holy Spirit to be with us forever.) Why did God send the Holy Spirit? (He enables us to understand the things of God, especially God's commandments.)

This was a fulfillment of Jesus' own prophecy when he said:

"But the Counselor, the Holy Spirit, whom the Father will send in my name, will teach you all things and will remind you of everything I have said to you" (John 14:26).

Call attention to the reading of Ruth.

Why is the book of Ruth read on Pentecost? (The book and the holiday both have the theme of the harvest.) Telling others about Jesus is like a being a harvester— bringing people into God's kingdom. Jesus said to his disciples

"The harvest is plentiful but the workers are few. Ask the Lord of the harvest, therefore, to send out workers into his harvest field" (Matthew 9:37, 38).

How can we be harvesters for Jesus?

Preparation

Read Exodus 19; Leviticus 23:15-21; Ruth 1—4; Acts 2:1-14, 40-42.

Gather supplies needed for crafts.
- ❑ drinking straws (2 per person)
- ❑ markers
- ❑ tape
- ❑ scissors
- ❑ yarn
- ❑ photocopies of pages 37, 38

Prepare cheese pastries. See page 36.

Decide how to present the application of this celebration.

The Celebration

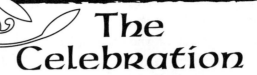

Tell the story of the giving of the *Torah*.

After the Israelites were freed from slavery in Egypt, they went into a desert wilderness. Fifty days after Passover, they camped at the base of Mt. Sinai. And when Moses went up on the mountain to talk to God, the Lord gave him the *Torah,* which is the Hebrew word for "instruction" or the Law. The *Torah* was 613 commandments from God that taught the people how to live cooperatively with one another. That meant if a person did something wrong to another person, everyone would know what the penalty would be. The *Torah* also showed them how to worship God. Part of the Law included the Ten Commandments.

The *Torah* revealed some things about God's holiness—he is separate from all creation, separate from all things that are not perfect like him. Because God is holy and people are not perfect, the people had a big problem. In fact, when Moses was up on the mountain, the other people were not allowed to go up there and be in the same place as God's holy presence. And there was thunder and lightning around the mountain that made the people tremble.

The *Torah* also revealed what sin was. It showed the ways that people commit wrongs, especially against God. So the *Torah* showed the people what was expected of them in order to have a relationship with a holy God. Later, when Moses wrote the first five books of the Bible; Genesis, Exodus, Leviticus, Numbers and Deuteronomy, he included all of these commandments for godly living as well as the history of ancient Israel.

Originally the Bible was written on long pieces of parchment, which is like paper, and attached to wooden rollers. Then as the words are read, the scroll is wound from one roller to the other. We are now going to make our own *Torah* scrolls that have Hebrew letters, the language of the Old Testament.

Make the _Torah_ scroll craft. See pages 37 and 38.

Say the blessings.
As participants stand, holding their scrolls, the leader says the following blessings:

"Bah-RUKE a-TAH ah-doe-NI el-o-HEY-nu MEL- eck ha-o-LAM ah-SHAIR BAH-har BAH-noo MEE-kol ha-ah-MEEM, veh NAH-tahn LAH-noo et TOE-rah-toe. Bah-RUKE a-TAH ah-doe- NI NO-tain ha-TOE-rah. Ah-MAIN."

"Blessed are you, O Lord our God, King of the universe who called us from the nations and has given us his _Torah_. Blessed are you, O Lord, who gave us the _Torah_. Amen."

"O Lord our God, you gave us holidays for gladness and seasons for rejoicing. You granted us this festival of Pentecost. We are grateful for your commandments, which you revealed at Sinai and fulfilled in Jesus the Messiah. Because of your goodness and your salvation, we will serve you truthfully. O Lord our God, may all of us praise you for blessing your people and for giving us the festivals. Amen."

Tell the story of Ruth.

Each year in Jewish synagogues, the book of Ruth is read on the holiday of Pentecost. Ruth was a Gentile, meaning she wasn't Jewish or from the nation of Israel. She was from the land of Moab where the true God was not worshiped. She married a Jewish man whose family had come to Moab to escape famine in Israel. But when her husband died, she went to the land of Israel along with her Jewish mother-in-law, Naomi.

Ruth said to Naomi, "Where you go I will go, and where you stay I will stay. Your people will be my people and your God my God" (Ruth 1:16). In Israel she began working in the harvest of the fields of a Jewish man named Boaz. He cared for her and eventually they became married. We also know that Ruth and Boaz later were the grandparents of king David.

Ruth was not born an Israelite, but she became one. That meant she was not born in a place that believed in the true God but became part of a nation that did believe in him.

One of the reasons that the book of Ruth is read on this day is because the story of Ruth takes place during harvest time and Pentecost also comes at the time of year when the grain farmers of Israel start to harvest grain. In the ancient days of the Bible, on the day of Pentecost the people of Israel were commanded by God to bring an offering of grain to the Lord. And they were to bring to the temple two loaves of bread that they had baked from this grain.

Tell the Pentecost story from the book of Acts.

There is one more thing to tell that explains the connection between the giving of the Law to Moses and the harvest story of Ruth.

As I said before, the Law revealed the ways that people sin. It also showed that not one person could ever keep the Law perfectly. As the Bible says, "For whoever keeps the whole law and yet stumbles at just one point is guilty of breaking all of it" (James 2:10).

Following the Law perfectly would be a very difficult thing for the people of Israel to do. And in the years to follow, no one could ever keep the Law without making one mistake. But God, who is loving in addition to being holy, would provide a way of escape. First he sent us his Son, Jesus, to die for our sins so that when we believe in him, the Law becomes perfected in our hearts. In other words, we can think and act in a godly way because God changes us for the better. He also did this by sending his Holy Spirit to be with us so that we can understand the things of God, including the Law.

We shouldn't be surprised to see the grand fulfillment of these things on the actual day of Pentecost that came fifty days after

Jesus died. The book of Acts (2:1-42) tells about how the Holy Spirit came in a powerful way on that special day of Pentecost. On that day alone 3,000 people from many different nations were saved. Like a harvest of grain, they were a spiritual harvest. Like the two loaves of bread offered to the Lord, Jewish and Gentile people come before God in exactly the same way, through faith in Jesus.

This is the message of Pentecost—that God, who is holy, desires to bring all people from the entire world into his family and to teach us his ways. And he fulfilled both of these things when he sent the Holy Spirit on the day of Pentecost. So when we believe in Jesus, we too can become part of God's harvest. And we too can have the Holy Spirit to help us live godly lives.

The Bible tells us that the Word of God is good for us like milk and sweet like honey. So on Pentecost traditional foods are sweet and include dairy products such as milk and cheese.

Present the application of this celebration to contemporary living. See pages 30, 31.

Traditional Cheese Pastries

Mini-Cheesecakes

1 1/2 cups graham cracker or chocolate wafer crumbs
1/4 cup sugar
1/4 cup margarine or butter (melted)
3 8-oz. packages cream cheese (softened)
1 14-oz. can sweetened condensed milk
3 eggs
2 teaspoons vanilla extract

Preheat oven to 300 degrees. Combine crumbs, sugar and margarine. Press equal portions on bottoms of paper-lined muffin cups. In large bowl, beat cheese until fluffy. Gradually beat in sweetened condensed milk until smooth. Add eggs and vanilla; mix well. Spoon equal amounts of mixture (about 3 tablespoons) into prepared cups. Bake 20 minutes or until tops spring back when lightly touched. Cool and refrigerate. Makes 24.

Cheese Knishes (cheese-filled cakes)

2 1/2 cups flour
2 1/2 teaspoons baking powder
1/2 teaspoon salt
2 eggs
1/2 cup sour cream
3 tablespoons melted butter
1/2 cup milk
1/2 lb. pot cheese
1 to 2 tablespoons bread crumbs
1 tablespoon sugar
1 tablespoon raisins

To make the dough: sift together dry ingredients. Beat 1 egg well, and add 1/4 cup sour cream. Stir into the dry ingredients. Add butter and part of the milk, stirring in more milk as needed to make a soft, but not sticky, dough. Roll out 1/8-inch thick on a floured board. Cut into three-to four-inch rounds or squares.

To make the filling: Mix together the remaining egg, 1/4 cup sour cream, pot cheese, crumbs, sugar and raisins. Place a spoonful on half of each square or round; fold dough over to cover. Press edges together with a fork. Bake on a greased baking sheet in a preheated oven (350 degrees) for 30 to 35 minutes (until brown). Makes 18.

Hebrew
Text
for
Torah
Scroll

Cut along dotted line.

Exodus 20:1-17

Materials for one scroll craft

- photocopies of pages 37, 38
- two straws
- pencils, crayons, or markers
- scissors
- adhesive tape

Torah Scroll and Cover

1. Cut out the Hebrew text (page 37) along the dotted line.
2. Tape each side of the cut page to a straw. (One piece of tape at the top and another at the bottom of each side works best.)

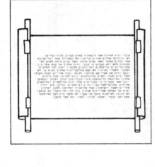

3. Cut out this *Torah* scroll cover. Color with pencils, crayons, or markers. Overlap and tape the ends of the cover together. Adjust the overlap to fit your scroll. A one-inch overlap usually works well.
4. Fold the long narrow tab over the top opening and tape to the opposite side (at the overlap).
5. Slide the cover over the scroll until it rests against the tab.

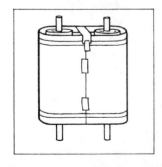

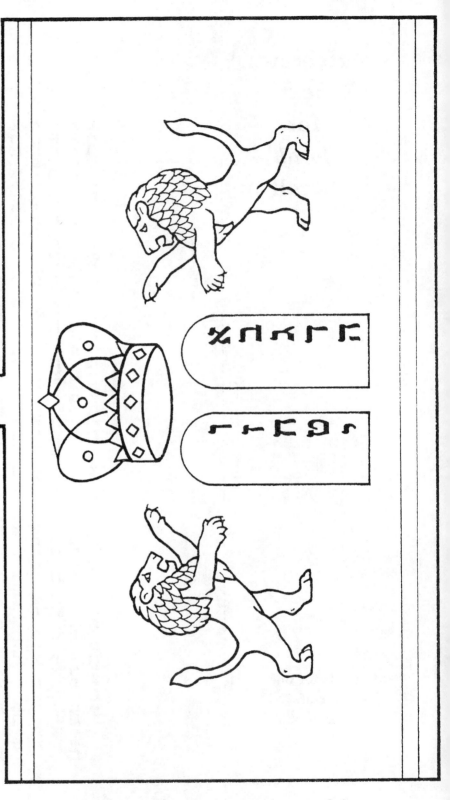

The scroll cover lists the first ten letters of the Hebrew alphabet. Each letter represents one of the Ten Commandments. Reading is begun in the upper right hand corner.

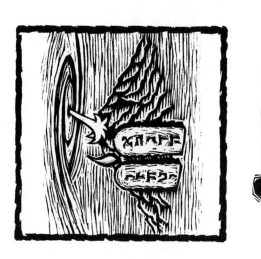

Come
Celebrate!

You are invited

to a

celebration

of

THE FEAST
of
PENTECOST

Date _____

Time _____

Place _____

The Feast  of Trumpets

Rosh Hashanah

BIBLICAL MONTH	*Tishri*
MODERN EQUIVALENT	September/October
O.T. REFERENCE	Leviticus 23:23-35; Numbers 29:1-6
N.T. REFERENCE	1 Thessalonians 4:16

An Overview

This is the first of the fall festivals. It is known in modern Jewish observance as *Rosh Hashanah* (rosh ha-SHAH-nah), which means "New Year." The central feature for this holiday is the *shofar* (SHO-far), a ram's horn. This feast teaches the purpose of trumpets in biblical days and demonstrates how the *shofar* is blown today. Using a real *shofar* or another type of horn, the special sound patterns are demonstrated. Afterward, a craft provides the opportunity for everyone to make a *shofar*. In keeping with the traditional observance, the story of Abraham and Isaac is told, and the Messianic symbolism is explained. Since it is customary to eat sweet foods on this holiday, apples dipped in honey are eaten during the refreshment time. Overall, we learn the importance of faithfulness to God and his provision of the Savior.

Biblical Heritage

Unlike the previous feasts, there is no specific event directly identified in Scripture that occurred on this day of the year. It was believed by ancient rabbis that the creation of the world began on this day and, as a result, it has been the practice to number the years of the Jewish calendar beginning from this date (reckoned to be over 5,700 years ago). But beyond their reasoning, we cannot be certain on this matter.

We do know a great deal about the principal feature of this feast—trumpets. In the culture of the Bible, trumpets were used to herald the beginning of each month at the first sighting of the new moon. In times of war they were used to signal armies whether to advance or retreat. They were also used as a call to assembly for the people of Israel. Whenever the Israelites needed to gather together as a body, the signal was the blowing of trumpets.

Historical Observance

The most significant assembly of all became the annual convocation outlined in Leviticus 23:23-35 and Numbers 29:1-6. The first day of the seventh month *(Tishri)* marked the beginning of the time for national repentance, culminating ten days later on the Day of Atonement. Trumpets were the signal to begin preparing for that coming judgment day. For that reason, in biblical times this feast was known as *Yom Teruah* (Yoam teh-ROO-ah, "Day of the Trumpet Sound"). This day had some specified burnt offerings by the priests, but for the people it was simply to be a time of rest and introspection, initiated by the blowing of the trumpets.

There is no reference in the Bible to this holiday as the New Year. Neither is it labeled in that manner in any historical books of the Second Temple period. However, shortly after the destruction of the temple, it is called *Rosh Hashanah*—

the beginning of the religious year (the month of *Nisan* was considered to be the beginning of the civil year). From that time onward, *Rosh Hashanah* became the common name of this feast.

Modern Observance

The blowing of the *shofar* continues to give *Rosh Hashanah* its primary character. The place of assembly is now the synagogue, where the religiously observant gather for services. It is said that the *shofar* is blown for three reasons. One is a reminder of God's command to Abraham to sacrifice Isaac. Thus Genesis 22 is customarily read. Another reason is to confuse Satan. Jewish legend holds that Satan seeks to bring charges against the Jewish people on this day and that the sound of the *shofar* prevents him from making accusations. The third reason for blowing trumpets on this day is a call to repentance. A special ceremony, called *tashlich* (tash-LEEK, meaning "cast off") takes place at a body of water where the people empty their pockets, symbolically casting away their sins.

A popular greeting for this holiday is translated, "May you be inscribed in the book for a good year." This custom comes from a rabbinical tradition that on *Rosh Hashanah* books are opened in Heaven. There is a book for the righteous, one for the not-so-righteous, and one for the wicked. The righteous are said to receive immediate blessings of prosperity and peace. The wicked are condemned to death. And those in between have until the Day of Atonement to receive blessing or condemnation. Since most people fall into this latter category, this becomes a serious need. With ten days until the Day of Atonement, people seek goodwill with one another and a sense of contrition before God.

Changes in Observance

In many ways, the modern observance of this holiday has retained most of its original character. There is a healthy sense of solemnity among observant Jews in reflection upon their lives. It is surely not the kind of "New Year" much of the world is used to celebrating on January 1. And while there may not be the complete assurance of lasting forgiveness (as compared to that provided by the sacrificial death of Messiah Jesus), we can commend the attitude of repentance modeled in this holiday.

When viewed on a different level, this is a feast that is yet to see its total fulfillment. For a day is coming when God will gather together his faithful ones to be with him throughout eternity. It will be a time that just precedes a final Day of Judgment. But it will also be a time that is heralded by the blowing of a *shofar*.

"For the Lord himself will descend from heaven with a shout, with the voice of the archangel and the trumpet of God; and the dead in Messiah will rise first. Then we who are alive and remain shall be caught up together with them in the clouds to meet the Lord in the air, and thus shall we always be with the Lord" (1 Thessalonians 4:16,17).

Note: The holiday *Rosh Hashanah* is not specifically mentioned in the New Testament.

Application

After sharing the stories of *Rosh Hashanah,* explore the symbolism of trumpets.

Why do you suppose this story is told each year on the Feast of Trumpets? (The *shofar* is a ram's horn.) This feast also looks to the future. A day is coming when God will call all who believe in Jesus to be with him forever (1 Thessalonians 4:16).

Therefore, just as the people of Israel prepared themselves to be judged by God on the Feast of Trumpets, when we go to be with the Lord in Heaven, he will judge us. He will look at our lives and will know everything about us. When that day comes, if we have believed in Jesus as our Savior, we will live with him in Heaven forever.

Talk about faithfulness to God.

Abraham had a hard choice to make. What was that choice? (Obey God and possibly lose Isaac or disobey God and possibly keep Isaac.)

What are some ways that we need to be faithful to God when we also feel like doing something else?

Choosing to obey God means knowing right from wrong. It means knowing what Jesus has told us in the Bible. Jesus said

"My sheep listen to my voice; I know them, and they follow me" (John 10:27).

Consider substitutionary sacrifice.

Do you think Abraham knew that God would provide another sacrifice (like the ram) instead of Isaac? (Notice what he said to his servants: "We will worship and then *we* will come back to you." God had made promises to Abraham; if he truly trusted God, then he believed that somehow God would provide a way out of this problem.)

When Abraham sacrificed the ram, it was a substitute for Isaac. What does that mean? (A sacrifice was required, but one dies in the place of another. This is what happened with Jesus. Because we all sin against God, we are guilty, but Jesus died in place of us for our sins.) As the Apostle Paul wrote

"But God demonstrates his own love for us in this: While we were still sinners, Christ died for us" (Romans 5:8).

Preparation

Read Leviticus 23:23-25; Genesis 22:1-19.

Obtain a *shofar* (borrow from a friend who has one or purchase one from a Jewish gift shop) or substitute a modern horn.

Practice blowing the *shofar* notes. See page 46.

Gather supplies needed for the trumpet craft.
- ❑ scissors
- ❑ tape
- ❑ glue
- ❑ glitter
- ❑ markers
- ❑ photocopies of the funnel on page 46 or obtain plastic funnels
- ❑ For each child, cut a paper tube, a PVC tube, or a flexible garden hose into 8-10 inch sections (make sure there are no ragged ends).

Prepare refreshments. Core and slice apples. Fill one or more bowls with honey for dipping the apples.

Decide how to present the application of this celebration to contemporary living.

The Celebration

Teach the purpose of trumpets in biblical days.

In the days of the Bible, there were two kinds of trumpets. There were long ones sometimes made out of silver, but most often made from the horns of rams and goats. This kind of a trumpet was called a *shofar*. The horns were hollowed out and shaped in different ways. Trumpets were used to call together the people of Israel. Whenever the people needed to be in the same place, the signal was the blowing of trumpets. It could be for times of war or approaching danger. And on the first day of every year, trumpets were blown in a special ceremony. Today this holiday is known as *Rosh Hashanah,* meaning "New Year." But in biblical days it was called the Feast of Trumpets.

The sound of trumpets at this feast was a signal for the people to prepare themselves for the Day of Atonement coming ten days later when God would forgive their sins. It was a time for them to think seriously about how they were living their lives.

A very special sound pattern was established for blowing the *shofar* on this day. The different notes are a long blast, a medium note, and a short fast note. So in the temple area on the Feast of Trumpets, many priests would stand and blow their *shofarim* (sho-far-EEM) something like this . . .

Blow the *shofar*.

Blow consecutively:

    1 long note

    3 medium notes (Try to undulate them: begin soft, end loud.)

    9 fast short notes (staccato)

    1 long note

            Repeat:

               1 long, 3 medium, 9 short, 1 long (as long as you can hold the last note!)

Make the trumpet craft.

Lead the children in singing.

An example of a song for this theme is "Make a Joyful Noise Unto the Lord" in the *Sing-a-Long Songbook* by Integrity Music.

Tell the story of Abraham and Isaac on Mt. Moriah.

One of the traditions for this holiday is the telling of a story that took place almost 3,000 years ago. It is about a man named Abraham who lived in the desert with his wife, Sarah. He believed in God and God blessed him for being faithful. After a long time of waiting for a son, God allowed Abraham and Sarah to have Isaac, and through this son a great nation was promised. In those days God spoke directly to certain people like Abraham, and one day God announced a test of faith for him.

God said, "Take your only son, Isaac, whom you love, and go to the land of Moriah. Offer him as a sacrifice there on one of the mountains I will tell you about." Now to sacrifice Isaac meant that Abraham would have to kill him, which you can imagine would be a horrible thing to do. Abraham was probably wondering why God would ask him to do such a thing and how God's promises would come about if Isaac were to die. But Abraham also knew that he had to obey God.

Early the next morning Abraham got up and saddled his donkey. He and Isaac, along with two servants, then left for the place God had told him about. Three days later Abraham looked up and saw the place in the distance. So he told his servants, "Stay here with the donkey while I and the boy go over there. We will worship and then we will come back to you."

As the two of them walked toward the mountain together, Isaac asked his father, "Where is the lamb for the sacrifice?"

Abraham answered, "God himself will provide the lamb, my son." And the two of them walked on together.

When they reached the place God had told him about, Abraham built an altar there and piled wood on it. An altar is a place where sacrifices are offered. Animals were normally killed on them and then burned in a fire. Abraham tied up his son Isaac and placed him on the altar, on top of the wood. Then he reached out his hand and took the knife to slay his son.

But the angel of the Lord called out to him from Heaven, "Abraham! Abraham!"

"Here I am," he answered.

"Do not do anything to the boy," the angel said. "Now I know that you believe in God, because you have trusted me with your only son."

Abraham looked up and saw a ram caught by its horns in some bushes. He went over and took the ram and sacrificed it as a burnt offering instead of his son. The ram became a substitute for Isaac. So Abraham called that place "The Lord Will Provide."

The angel of the Lord called to Abraham from Heaven again and said, "Because you have trusted me, I will bless you and make your descendants as numerous as the stars in the sky and as the sand on the seashore. And all people on earth will be blessed because you have obeyed me."

These things that were promised happened exactly the way that God said they would. Later, this same mountain called Moriah is where the temple and the city of Jerusalem were built. And the nation of Israel grew from Abraham's family. Many millions of people were born, starting with Isaac. But that's not all. Most importantly, one of those descendants was Jesus. It was Jesus who came to bring salvation to the whole world. That's what the angel meant when he said all people on earth would be blessed. Salvation was coming to the world through one of Abraham's descendants— Jesus. Like Isaac, Jesus was the only Son of his Father. Like Isaac, Jesus was offered as a sacrifice. And like Isaac, God gave back Jesus alive when he was resurrected from the dead.

So there are two very important lessons to be learned from this story. Just as Abraham was faithful to God, we too need to obey him and to trust him to take care of us. And Abraham's willingness to offer his son Isaac as a sacrifice is a clue about what would happen in the life of Jesus many years later.

Present the application of this celebration to contemporary living. See page 44.

Enjoy the apples and honey.

Another tradition on this holiday is eating apples and honey. Since this day happens on the first day of the Jewish calendar, it is a way of hoping for a sweet new year.

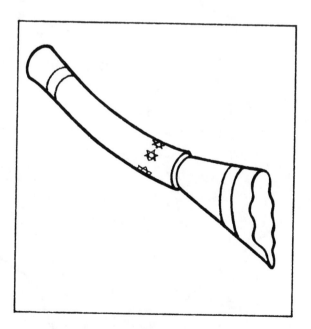

Trumpet

Materials for one trumpet craft
- a funnel or a photocopy of the pattern on this page
- 8-to-10-inch paper tube, PVC tube or flexible garden hose
- glue
- glitter and markers
- scissors
- adhesive tape
- option: adhesive-backed plastic

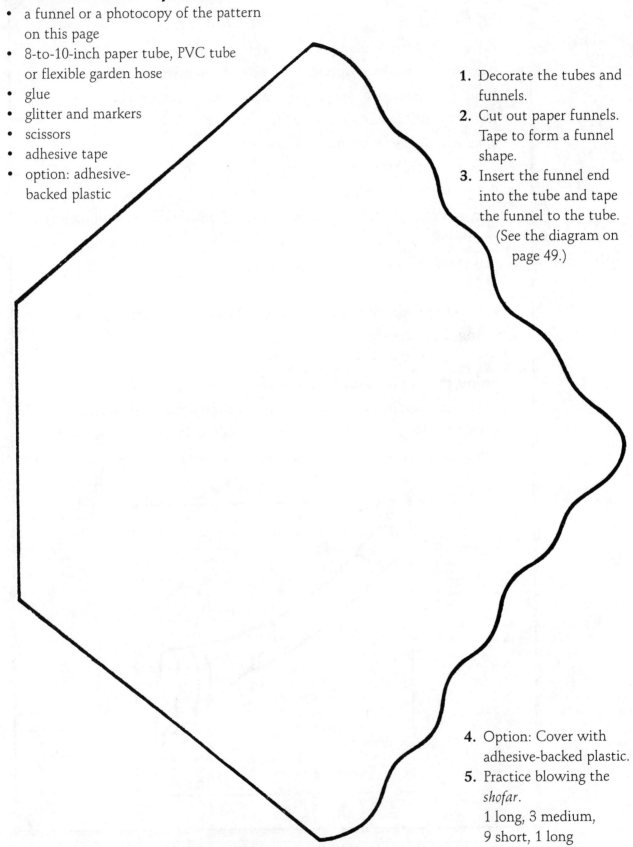

1. Decorate the tubes and funnels.
2. Cut out paper funnels. Tape to form a funnel shape.
3. Insert the funnel end into the tube and tape the funnel to the tube. (See the diagram on page 49.)

4. Option: Cover with adhesive-backed plastic.
5. Practice blowing the *shofar*.
   1 long, 3 medium, 9 short, 1 long

A Celebration

Please Come

You are invited to
a celebration of . . .

THE FEAST
OF
TRUMPETS

Date

Time

Place

The Day of Atonement

Yom Kippur

BIBLICAL MONTH	*Tishri*
MODERN EQUIVALENT	September/October
O.T. REFERENCE	Leviticus 16:1-34; 23:26-28
N.T. REFERENCE	Hebrews 9:11—10:22; 13:11, 12

An Overview

With an emphasis on the temple and the priesthood, the leader tells the story about the high priest in the days of the tabernacle and temple. Then participants make a *kippah* (KIP-pah)—a hat which signifies reverence for God and also illustrates the principal of having a covering applied to our lives. Additional elements include a song, refreshments, and one final blast of the *shofar.* Through this holiday, we learn how Jesus' death was an atonement made on our behalf once and for all, and recall the importance of having forgiveness in our lives.

Biblical Heritage

The awesome holiness of God permeates the background of this holiday. To be holy literally means to be "separate." God, who is pure and perfect, is separate from all things impure and imperfect. And in the course of establishing fellowship with humanity, he decreed that all people who draw near to him must likewise become holy (Leviticus 20:7). This holiness can only be imputed or given by God, not created by our own abilities.

The problem we face is that we sin, meaning we violate God's standards of holiness. And God made it clear, the penalty for sin is death (Ezekiel 18:20; Romans 6:23). But in his grace and love, God's way of providing holiness and fellowship with him on earth, and throughout eternity, was substitutionary sacrifice. In other words, people who sin and become impure, and are therefore guilty before God, can become pardoned and pure and therefore holy before God when the penalty of death is paid by another. This was the purpose for instituting the sacrificial system during the days of the tabernacle in the wilderness and later in the temple in Jerusalem. The shedding of blood was done to cover the sins of the people, as if the sins no longer exist (Leviticus 17:11; Psalm 32:1). The Hebrew word for "covering" is the root for this essential concept of atonement.

As part of this system, God ordained priests to manage the sacrifices and the other facets of biblical worship. From among these priests was set aside one individual known as the high priest who would assume the most significant task of all—representing the people of Israel before God in atoning for their sins.

Historical Observance

One day each year was designated as a national judgment day in Israel, called *Yom Kippur,* (yoam kip-POOR), the "Day of Atonement." It came ten days after the Feast of Trumpets and five days before the Feast of Tabernacles.

According to Leviticus 16, on this day the high priest first made atonement for himself through prescribed sacrifices and rituals. He then sacrificed a bull and took some of the blood past the double curtains into the Holy of Holies, the one room in the tabernacle and later in the temple that was off-limits to all people except the high priest on this single day. There he sprinkled the blood on the ark of the covenant which housed the sacred artifacts—the stone tablets of the Ten Commandments, a pot of manna, and Aaron's rod that budded.

Outside once more, the high priest took two goats and cast lots to determine the fate of the animals. He took one goat and slaughtered it. Blood from this goat was then sprinkled on the ark as before, plus on other places in the sanctuary. This sprinkling of the blood was the actual act of atonement. The second goat was symbolically given the sins of the people. A red sash was tied around its horns, and it was sent away into the wilderness, representing the sins of the people being sent away. The red sash would turn to white as a sign of God's approval of the atonement ceremonies. These rituals were carried out essentially in the same manner in the tabernacle and the temple.

Meanwhile, the people prepared themselves spiritually for this day, culminating with a fast on *Yom Kippur*. The Hebrew expression for fasting is "afflicting the soul" (alternatively translated as "denying oneself"). This was the primary responsibility of the general population on the Day of Atonement (Leviticus 23:29).

Modern Observance

The attributes of today's commemoration of *Yom Kippur* are personal repentance, prayer, fasting, and acts of charity. Fasting is emphasized as a demonstration of one's penitence. It is also commonly stated that there is no longer a need for an intermediary like the high priest because now a person can go directly to God. Some orthodox Jews today perform a ceremony in which a fowl is waved over one's head and slaughtered as a transferal of sins, but this practice is not widely observed.

In synagogue services one traditional prayer is the *Kol Nidre* (cole NEE-dray, "All Vows"), a custom dating back to the time when the Spanish inquisition imposed baptism on many Jews or condemned them to be burned at the stake. Many Jewish people responded with the *Kol Nidre* which renounces "all the vows of water and fire." This prayer is a sad testimony to the historical suffering of the Jews.

Other practices include a memorial service for close relatives, the reading of the book of Jonah (a story depicting the Lord as the God of all nations), and a final blast of the *shofar* (ram's horn) to signal the end of fasting.

Changes in Observance

The destruction of the temple in A.D. 70 completely eliminated the sacrificial system of Israel. In the subsequent years, rabbinical Judaism redefined the way that the Day of Atonement was to be observed. No longer would there be a priesthood and sacrifices. No longer would there be a personal encounter with a holy God. In its place have emerged atonement through prayer and fasting. But by biblical definition, this is not atonement—"for it is the blood that makes atonement for one's life" (Leviticus 17:11).

The ancient Jewish commentary *Talmud* acknowledges that something dramatic happened even before the fall of the temple that impacted the Day of Atonement:

> Forty years before the holy temple was destroyed, the lot of the *Yom Kippur* ceased to be supernatural; the red cord of wool that used to change white now remained red and did not change . . . *(Yoma 39b)*.

What happened forty years before the fall of the temple? It was the death of Jesus on or around A.D. 30. This was the final, perfect substitutionary sacrifice. His shed blood would cover the sins of all who receive this free gift. And unlike the high priests who had to return year after year, repeating the prescribed sacrifices, Messiah "entered the Most Holy Place once for all by his own blood, having obtained eternal redemption" (Hebrews 9:12). The temple and the high priest served no further purpose. When Jesus died on the cross, the sign of God's granting of atonement—the changing of the red sash of the scapegoat to white—no longer was given. Shortly thereafter, the temple itself became a pile of rubble and the people were dispersed. But the lasting atonement provided by Jesus carries on (Hebrews 9:11—10:22).

Application

Before concluding the celebration, review the events on the Day of Atonement.
How many times each year did the high priest go into the Holy of Holies? (One.) What was the meaning of sending away the scapegoat? (The sins of the people were sent away. They were forgiven.) When we believe in Jesus, all of our sins are sent away like that. King David once said

> *"As far as the east is from the west, so far has he removed our transgressions from us"* (Psalm 103:12).

Discuss the concepts of atonement and forgiveness.
What does the word "atonement" mean? (Covering our sins.) Another way of thinking about what happens when we believe in Jesus is that our sins are covered over—you can't see them anymore. As the apostle Paul wrote

> *"Blessed are they whose transgressions are forgiven, whose sins are covered"* (Romans 4:7).

Why is the atonement that comes from Jesus better than the atonement that came in the temple? (The temple atonement had to be repeated every year, but the atonement of Jesus lasts forever.) The Bible tells us

> *"Unlike the other high priests, he does not need to offer sacrifices day after day, first for his own sins, and then for the sins of the people. He sacrificed for their sins once for all when he offered himself"* (Hebrews 7:27).

If we understand what God has done for us, what should our attitude be?

Explain the custom of fasting.

One of the customs of the Day of Atonement has been fasting. That means people do not eat on this day. The purpose of fasting has been to help people think about what they have done during the past year and to tell God about it. This is called confession. While we don't have to fast today, some people choose to do so as a way of concentrating on God and his teachings. And while we are forgiven of our sins, it is important to confess our sins to God. It's good to know that any time we make a mistake and sin, God will hear our prayers and forgive us.

Blow the *shofar* with one long blast.

A custom that signals the end of the fast on the Day of Atonement is one last blowing of the trumpet called the *shofar*. Afterward, we will enjoy some refreshments. If you believe in Jesus as your Savior, as the *shofar* is blown, let it be a sign to you that your sins are forgiven forever.

Preparation

Read Leviticus 16:1-34; 23:26-28.

Obtain a *shofar* (ram's horn) or substitute a modern horn.

Gather supplies for the *kippah* craft.

☐ scissors　　　　　　☐ glue

☐ tape　　　　　　☐ stapler

☐ two pieces of construction paper or colored paper per child (each sheet should be a different color)

Prepare refreshments.

Decide how to present the application of this celebration to contemporary living.

The Celebration

Begin by telling the story of the high priest on the biblical Day of Atonement.

In biblical times, ten days after the people of Israel celebrated the Feast of Trumpets, they were called to keep another holy day. The Hebrew name is *Yom Kippur,* which means the Day of Atonement. It was the most important day of the year because that was when the sins of the people were forgiven.

One person was responsible for doing the service on this day. He was called the high priest. He was chosen from among the many priests who served in the worship in the temple in Jerusalem. He wore white linen clothes with a breastplate on his chest containing precious stones. His head was covered by a cap marked with the words, "Holy to the Lord."

The Day of Atonement was the only day during the year when anyone could enter the Holy of Holies—the special place in the temple where God's glorious presence appeared. And it was only the high priest who could go in the Holy of Holies. He first entered with burning incense, the smoke of which represented the prayers of the people rising up to God. The high priest then sacrificed a young bull for his own sins and went back into the Holy of Holies. There he sprinkled some of the blood from the young bull on the ark of the covenant, which was a gold-covered box with figures of angels on top.

Then two goats were brought to the high priest outside the temple. One goat was selected to be the sacrificial goat. The blood of this goat was offered by the high priest in the Holy of Holies for the sins of all the people of Israel. The priest went back outside and placed his hands on the head of the other goat, called the scapegoat.

Then it was sent far away from the people into the wilderness. This represented sending away all of the sins of the people. They were now forgiven. God no longer held the people responsible for their past sins and they would not be punished for them.

The Day of Atonement was God's way of forgiving the sins of the people of Israel. There are four important things for us to remember about this ancient ceremony. First, it had to be done exactly in the way God had ordered it. Second, it had to be done by one special person, the high priest, who had to be considered free of sin before he could act for the rest of the people. Third, when the people were forgiven, their past sins were sent away and could not be held against them again. But, fourth, this forgiveness did not cover any sins that they did afterward. There would have to be another Day of Atonement the next year, and the year after that, and so on.

What was it about sprinkling blood on the ark of the covenant that had to do with forgiveness? God has said that when we sin, we deserve punishment. But we are freed from that punishment when something is put between our sin and God. So when God looks upon us, he sees the blood sacrifice, not our sin. Our sin has been covered. That's what the word "atonement" means. Atonement is the covering of our sins.

The Hebrew word for atonement or covering is *kippur.* There is another similar Hebrew word, *kippah,* which is the name of a small cap that is worn as a sign of respect for God. It is a daily reminder of our need for forgiveness which comes from the covering of our sin.

So we are going to make our own *kippah* to help us remember the importance of forgiveness and also about the high priest who wore a cap on his head. Another word for this cap is a *yarmulke* (YAR-mul-kah).

Make the *kippah* craft.

Lead the group in singing.

An example of a song for this theme is "Come Into the Holy of Holies" in the *Sing-a-Long Songbook* by Integrity Music.

Explain how Jesus became our high priest.

What do you suppose was the biggest problem about the Day of Atonement in Bible times? Well, when this ceremony was followed according to God's instructions, it did what he said it would do. The sins of the people of Israel were forgiven. But the problem was that it had to be repeated every year. The ceremony would cover only the sins up to that day. It had to be done over and over again.

So God said there would be a better way. He would send his Son, Jesus, to fulfill two very important parts of atonement. The death of Jesus would satisfy the need for sacrifice and he would also be the last high priest. Because he lived a perfect life without ever sinning once, his sacrifice would be perfect—it would be the last one ever needed. In fact, soon after Jesus died, the temple was destroyed by the Romans—never to be rebuilt again. So today there is no longer a temple or priests to lead the worship as in biblical days. But because of what Jesus did for us, we actually no longer need them.

Jesus became our atonement. He has covered over our sins forever. We don't have to worry about needing another Day of Atonement next year. And like the high priest of Israel, he has done the entire work of salvation for us. All we have to do is believe in him and receive his gift of salvation.

Present the application of this celebration to contemporary living. See page 56.

"Break the fast" by enjoying refreshments.

One option is to obtain *hallah* (HALL-ah), a traditional Jewish bread eaten at most Sabbath and holiday gatherings. *Hallah* can be purchased at many bakeries and grocery stores. Or you can provide some cookies, such as this traditional recipe:

Honey Cookies

Ingredients

3 eggs
1 1/4 cups sugar
3/4 cup honey
4 cups flour
1 teaspoon cinnamon
1/4 teaspoon baking soda

Beat eggs until light. Add sugar gradually while beating. Beat in the honey gradually. Add sifted dry ingredients and mix well. Drop mixture from a teaspoon onto a cookie sheet lined with ungreased wrapping paper. Bake at 300 degrees for 15 minutes. Do not brown. Remove to cooling rack while warm. Makes eight dozen.

A *Kippah* Cap

Materials for one *kippah*

- 2 sheets of colored paper per child
- adhesive tape or glue
- staples
- scissors

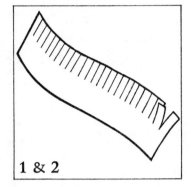

1. Fold one sheet of colored paper in half along the long edge and cut along the fold. Tape or staple the two pieces into one strip approximately 4 1/2 inches wide by 22 inches long.
2. Cut slits halfway across the strip spaced about one to two inches apart.

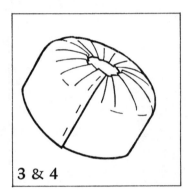

3. Place the strip of paper on the head of a child and wrap around until ends meet. Remove the cap while holding the ends together for an exact fit and staple the ends on the overlap. Tape over the staples.
4. Bend the tabs to the inside and staple, glue or tape together. This will form the top of the cap, but will leave a space in the center.

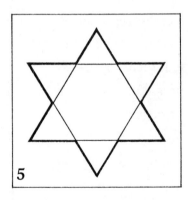

5. Draw two overlapping equilateral triangles on the second sheet of paper. Each side of the triangle should measure five to six inches. The resulting star should be slightly smaller than the diameter of the cap. Cut out the star.

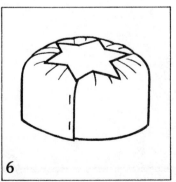

6. Glue or tape the star on the top of the cap, with the lines from the triangles on the underside.

fold forward

You are invited to a remembrance for

The Day
of
Atonement

fold back

_____

Date

_____

Time

_____

Place

_____

Please Come

The Feast

of

Tabernacles

Sukkot

BIBLICAL MONTH	*Tishri*
MODERN EQUIVALENT	September/October
O.T. REFERENCE	Leviticus 23:33-36, 39-44
N.T. REFERENCE	John 7:2—9:5

An Overview

The theme of this holiday is a reminder that the journey of the Israelites through the wilderness was a temporary one and that their ultimate dwelling place would be with God in the land of Israel. In this observance everyone helps build and decorate a temporary shelter called a *sukkah* (SOO–kah), meaning "tabernacle" or "booth." Thus the Hebrew name for this holiday is *Sukkot* (soo–COAT), meaning "tabernacles." Then the tabernacle is blessed and some can "dwell" in it, eating their refreshments and singing a song. Everyone hears about the symbolism of our future dwelling place with God in Heaven.

Biblical Heritage

After the Israelites were delivered from bondage in Egypt and given the Law on Mt. Sinai, it would be forty years before they would settle in the promised land of Canaan. It was during this interim period that they lived as nomads, traveling the arid desert and mountains of the south and dwelling in portable tents. God used a pillar of cloud to lead them by day and a pillar of fire by night (Exodus 13:21). Scripture tells us that "Whenever the cloud lifted from above the Tent, the Israelites set out; wherever the cloud settled, the Israelites encamped" (Numbers 9:17). And so it went for forty years—the people dwelling in temporary structures in the midst of God's presence.

Historical Observance

God instructed the descendants of Israel to commemorate the wilderness wanderings of their ancestors in the annual Feast of Tabernacles (Leviticus 23:42, 43). The Hebrew word *sukkah* is translated "tabernacle, booth, or hut" and is not to be confused with the tabernacle (also known as the Tent of Meeting) that housed the Holy of Holies and where the divine presence of God resided.

In temple times, five days after the Day of Atonement, the people were to begin dwelling in *sukkot* (the plural form of the word). They were to do so for a period of one week (Leviticus 23:41, 42). In the context of God's instructions is a command to "take choice fruit from the trees, and palm fronds, leafy branches, poplars, and rejoice before the Lord your God for seven days" (Leviticus 23:40). The Sadducees interpreted this verse to mean that the tree branches were to be used on the *sukkot*. But the Pharisees said that the branches were to be carried by the people. The solution was a compromise. Branches would be placed as roofs on the booths and the various types of tree branches would be placed together in what is called a *lulav* (LOO–lahv) and waved by the people in the temple courtyard. In addition, the "choice fruit" was said to mean the *etrog* (EH–trog), a native citrus fruit known as the citron.

This holiday was the third and final pilgrimage festival (Exodus 23:14–17). Thus the people of Israel would come from everywhere to Jerusalem, singing the Psalms of Ascent (120–134) along the way. Upon their arrival they would set up their booths with leafy roofs and live in them for seven days. With booths set up in every open courtyard and on the roofs of houses, the entire city was adorned in greenery.

Each day in the temple, special ceremonies took place. Animals were sacrificed, as in other feasts, but unique to this festival was the "pouring of water" ritual. A priest would draw water from the spring of Siloam and return to the temple where he would march around the altar of sacrifice and pour out the water upon it. This would be done in the presence of the people, each person holding a *lulav* and an *etrog,* to the accompaniment of priests blowing silver trumpets and others singing God's praises.

In the evening came ceremonies involving brilliant lights in the temple's vast Court of Women. Massive candelabras were set up with large bowls of flaming oil that illuminated the entire city. On the courtyard men danced with torches and sang while the Levites played instruments of harps, psaltries, cymbals, flutes and trumpets.

On the seventh and final day of this festival, the people would shake their branches to the point of casting the leaves to the pavement and the children would eat the citron fruit. This day was called *Hoshana Rabba* (ho–SHAH–nah RAH–bah), meaning "the great hosanna." The name is derived from Psalm 118 in which the people would chant, "O Lord, save us" (verse 25). On the following day, the celebrations ceased and the people observed a special sabbath—a much needed day of rest.

Modern Observance

There are many similarities between the biblical and contemporary celebrations of *Sukkot.* Observant Jewish families erect booths outside their homes, with a minimum of three walls and at least half of the roof covered by branches. The most common custom is to eat meals in the *sukkah,* unless heavy rain chases the family indoors. Some people will also sleep in them during the seven days. Synagogues from the Reform branch of Judaism will also place a *sukkah* inside the synagogue during the holiday.

Services are characterized by the carrying of the *lulav* and the *etrog* and the performing of rites that echo biblical times. These rites include the encircling of the altar of sacrifice by the priests, during which the *Torah* scroll is highlighted. And like the pouring of water ceremony, the hands of the elders of congregations are washed.

After the Feast of Tabernacles is concluded, an additional holiday known as *Simhat Torah* (SIM-hot TOE-rah, "Rejoicing in the Law") is observed. This day marks the ending of the annual cycle of the *Torah* by reading the last chapter of Deuteronomy, and the beginning of a new cycle by reading the first chapter of Genesis.

Changes in Observance

On the surface, there is much faithfulness in the modern observance to the biblical instructions. But greatly overlooked in the festive nature of this holiday is its original intent—the people were to be reminded of the importance of dwelling with God. In ancient times it was a holiday that portrayed the God of Israel as one who seeks to fellowship with his people. To those who were looking for the fulfillment of God's promises, it would not have been a surprise to see these truths revealed on the very moment of the Feast of Tabernacles. For it was Jesus, God incarnate (Isaiah 9:6, 7), who said this about himself on *Sukkot*

> *"On the last and greatest day of the Feast, Jesus stood and said in a loud voice, 'If anyone is thirsty, let him come to me and drink. Whoever believes in Me, as the Scripture has said, streams of living water will flow from within him'" (John 7:37, 38).*

His words reflected upon the water imagery of *Sukkot*. And in keeping with the holiday symbol of light, he declared, "I am the light of the world" (John 9:5). Finally, his name, which means "the salvation of the Lord," is the answer to the *hoshana rabba* plea, "O Lord, save us."

The temporary nature of the *sukkah* is a vivid symbol of life here on earth. It is fragile and soon to be no more. But the stars that can be seen through the open spaces of the roof remind us of eternity and a permanent dwelling place with God. For believers in Jesus, all those who have received his salvation through faith in him, this is assurance. And one day this time of everlasting dwelling together will be the ultimate fulfillment of the Feast of Tabernacles.

Application

After building and experiencing the *sukkah*, explain the symbolism of the *sukkah*.

The temporary shelter of the *sukkah* is very much like our lives. We "wander" in a world that is sometimes like a wilderness. It's not always an easy place in which to live. The apostle Paul said

> *"Now we know that if the earthly tent we live in is destroyed, we have a building from God, an eternal house in heaven, not built by human hands" (2 Corinthians 5:1).*

Our bodies are not perfect. What does that mean? (They're not always totally strong and we won't live forever here on earth.) Paul also said

> *"For while we are in this tent, we groan and are burdened, because we do not wish to be unclothed but to be clothed with our heavenly dwelling, so that what is mortal may be swallowed up by life" (2 Corinthians 5:4).*

Talk about the symbolism of our eternal hope in this feast.

In the same way that God wanted the Israelites to live with him in the Promised Land, he wants us to live with him one day in Heaven. So if you can imagine yourself living in this booth out in the desert in the middle of the night, the stars shining through the roof would remind you that one day we will live with God forever in our permanent home in Heaven. What has Jesus promised us?

"In my Father's house are many rooms; if it were not so, I would have told you. I am going there to prepare a place for you. And if I go and prepare a place for you, I will come back and take you to be with me that you also may be where I am" (John 14:2, 3).

If we have this kind of hope, how will this make it easier for us to deal with problems today?

Preparation

Read Leviticus 23:33–36, 39–44.

Gather materials for the *sukkah* ("tabernacle" or "booth"). See the suggestions on page 73.

Prepare refreshments. In order to fulfill the command to "live in tabernacles," provide a snack to be eaten in the *sukkah*. Citrus fruit would be ideal.

Decide how to present the application of this celebration to contemporary living.

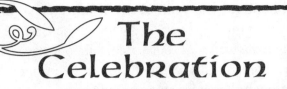

The Celebration

Tell the story as you build a *sukkah*.

Long ago when the people of Israel wandered in the wilderness for forty years, they lived in temporary homes. That means the houses were very simple and had to be moved many times. And when the people finally settled in the land of Canaan, God wanted them to remember those days in the wilderness. So he told them to observe this holiday called the Feast of Tabernacles once a year.

Each family was commanded to build a temporary shelter called a *sukkah,* meaning a "tabernacle'" or a "booth." And they were to live in them for seven days. God said, "Live in booths for seven days . . . so your descendants will know that I had the Israelites live in booths when I brought them out of Egypt" (Leviticus 23:42, 43).

So today we are going to build our own *sukkah* as part of our celebration.

If you decided to decorate the walls *before* they are attached, children can draw pictures on the siding. Pictures of buildings from Bible days or trees and flowers are ideal.

Organize the children in work crews and attach the walls to the *sukkah*. Place the roof on the *sukkah*.

God told the people that when they built their tabernacle, they were to use branches of trees. So one of the customs is to put green branches on the roof of the *sukkah*."

According to tradition, spaces are left between the branches so that you can look through to the sky.

Place the lattice, bamboo poles, or blanket on top, followed by the greenery.

Finish the roof with the branches. Decorate the *sukkah*.

If you decided to decorate the walls *after* they are attached, children can draw pictures of buildings from Bible days or trees and flowers on the siding.

Make the following crafts and hang them from the roof inside the *sukkah*.

• Add paper chains (stapled loops made of strips of construction paper linked into chains).

• Add paper fruit. Color the fruit on the photocopied pages and cut into individual pieces. Fashion the paper clips into hooks and attach some yarn to the clip and the fruit for hanging.

After the *sukkah* is completed, the leader says the traditional blessing.

"Ba-RUKE a-TAH ah-doe-NI el-o-HEY-nu MEL-eck ha-o-LAM ah-SHAIR kid-SHAH-noo bih MITS-vo-tahv vit-zee-VAH-noo, le-YEH-shave ba-SOO-kah."

"Blessed are you, O Lord our God, King of the universe, who has sanctified us by Your commandments, and has instructed us to dwell in the *sukkah*."

Lead the group in singing. An ideal choice is "The Children Cry Hosanna" in the *Sing-a-Long Songbook* by Integrity Music.

One of the customs of the Feast of Tabernacles during the days of the Bible, was called the *Hoshana Rabba* (ho-SHAH-nah RAH-bah), meaning the "the great hosanna" or "the great plea for salvation." The people would wave branches on this holiday and sing the words "Hosanna, hosanna."

Present the application of this celebration to contemporary living. See page 68.

Enjoy the refreshments.

In order to fulfill God's instruction to live in the *sukkah,* we will now do something that is part of living—eating food! (If the group is small, have all of them sit inside the *sukkah.* Larger groups may have to take turns, or some can sit in front.)

A *Sukkah*

Materials for Constructing a *Sukkah*

- framing lumber (2 x 2s or 2 x 4s)
- nails or screws
- siding (plywood, cardboard, fabric, newsprint)
- lattice or bamboo poles
- real or artificial branches
- scissors
- adhesive tape

paper chains
- construction paper cut into strips
- stapler

paper fruit and pictures
- photocopy of fruit page 74
- crayons or markers
- paper clips
- yarn
- blank paper

Assemble a *Sukkah*

Before the celebration, hammer or screw together a frame using four upright and eight horizontal pieces (cut to length according to space and material).

During the celebration, put the siding on three of the sides. Participants place lattice or bamboo poles across the top and then cover them with branches.

You can see through the roof of a proper *sukkah*, but there should be slightly more branches than space.

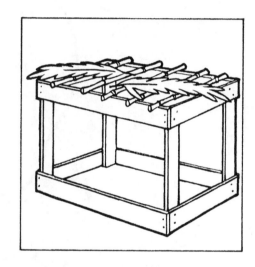

An Instant *Sukkah*

Turn an eight–foot rectangular table on its side. Add a sheet or blanket, leaving the front open. Place greenery on top.

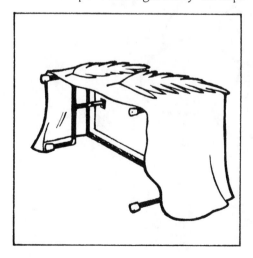

Improvise a *Sukkah*

Make a temporary shelter. You need a three-sided structure (an existing wall can serve as one side) with a leafy roof.

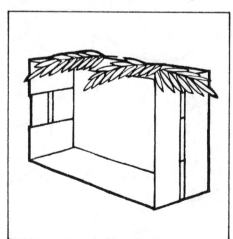

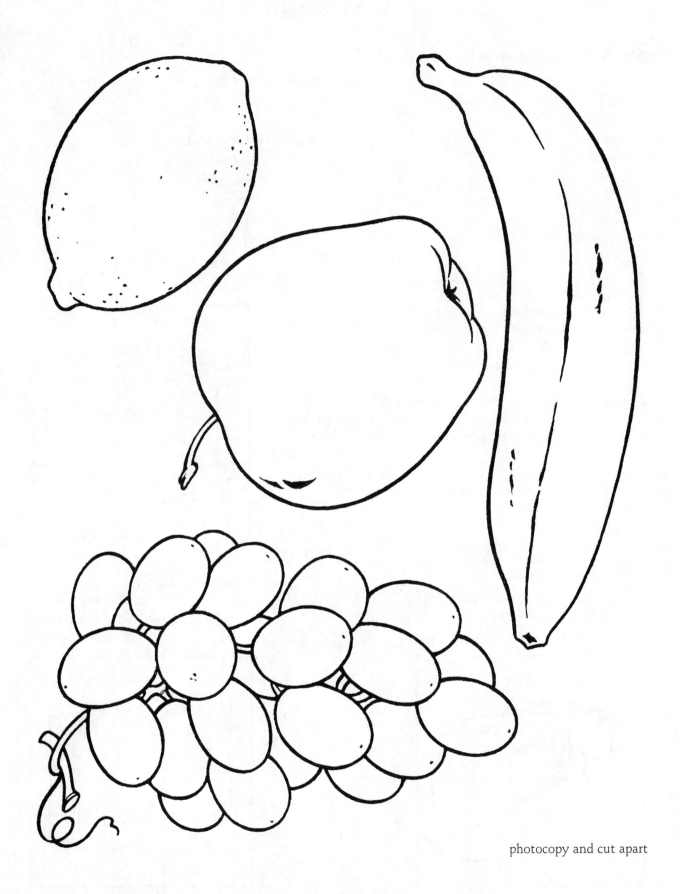

photocopy and cut apart

Please Come

*You are invited
to a celebration of*

**THE FEAST OF
TABERNACLES**

Date

Time

Place

The Feast

of

Dedication

Hanukkah

BIBLICAL MONTH	*Kislev*
MODERN EQUIVALENT	November/December
N.T. REFERENCE	John 10:22, 23

An Overview

The holiday of *Hanukkah* (HA-noo-kah) traces its origin to the time between the writing of the Old and New Testaments. The story is about a group of Jews known as the Maccabees (MAC-ah-bees) defeating the Syrians who had defiled the temple in Jerusalem. As participants light candles on the *Hanukkah menorah* (men-NO-rah), they hear about the miracle of *Hanukkah*. After making a holiday craft, they also sing, play the traditional *dreidel* (DRAY-del) game and enjoy some holiday foods. Through the symbolism of this holiday, participants learn about the miracle of Jesus—the light of the world—and the importance of servanthood in their lives.

Historical and Biblical Heritage

In the Old Testament, when the story of Nehemiah's return to Jerusalem concludes, there is a period of over 400 years of unrecorded history. During this 400 years before the New Testament record begins some significant events happened. One is the story of *Hanukkah*.

In order to discover what took place at that time, we must turn to the books of the Maccabees. These are some of the Apocryphal books not considered to be on the same level of divine inspiration as the Bible. The book of First Maccabees, however, is considered quite reliable as a historical source. It is a book that recalls what occurred in the land of Israel around 165 B.C. and is our principal reference for *Hanukkah*.

Prior to that time, Israel had been under the occupation of Greece, which was ruled by Alexander the Great. His death lead to the division of the empire and Israel became a territory of the Syrians. From this kingdom arose an immoral ruler named Antiochus Epiphanes (an-TIE-o-cuss eh-PIF-ah-nees). One of his objectives was to transform the Jewish society into a Hellenized one. In other words, he endeavored to make Israel like the rest of the "modern" Greek world.

> The king (Antiochus) sent letters by messengers unto Jerusalem and the cities of Judah, that they should follow the strange laws of the land, and forbid burnt offerings, sacrifice and drink offerings in the temple and that they should profane the sabbath and festival days. And they should pollute the sanctuary and holy people by setting up altars and chapels of idols, and they should sacrifice the flesh of swine and other unclean beasts. They should also leave their children uncircumcised and make their own souls abominable with all manner of profanation, to the end that they might forget the Law and change all the ordinances (1 Maccabees 1:44-49, 43).

Antiochus established a Greek city on the temple mount in Jerusalem and a statue of Zeus was placed in the temple itself. The gods of the Greek pantheon were to be worshiped. And as an insult to Jewish principles, a pig was sacrificed on the altar.

Many of the Israelites consented to the religion of Antiochus. They sacrificed to idols and profaned the Sabbath. Many Jewish people adopted Hellenistic changes. They took Greek names and set aside the practice of circumcision. Schools began teaching in the philosophy of Greek rationalism and Greek athletics became popular. For all intents and purposes—after surviving for many centuries—the biblical culture of Israel was being eliminated in a short period of time.

> But some in Israel were fully resolved and chose to die rather than to be defiled or to profane the holy covenant. And in those days arose a priest named Mattathias. When he saw the blasphemies that were committed, Mattathias answered and said with a loud voice, "Even though all the nations obey him, I and my sons will walk in the covenant of our fathers. God forbid that we should forsake the Law and the ordinances" (1 Maccabees 1:62, 63; 2:6, 19-21).

When this priest named Mattathias died, his son Judah led a resistance movement against the Syrians. These rebels, known as the Maccabees, were joined by other Jewish people who sought to return to their biblical way of life. Three years of struggle eventually led to victory by the Maccabees. After Jerusalem was reclaimed in battle:

> Judah said to his brothers, "Our enemies are defeated. Let us go up to cleanse and dedicate the Sanctuary." So he chose priests who were blameless to cleanse the Sanctuary and to take away the defiled stones to another location. Then they took whole stones, according to the Law, and built a new altar. They also made new holy vessels and into the Temple they brought the *menorah*, and the altar of incense and the table. And on the twenty-fifth day of *Kislev*, they offered sacrifice according to the Law upon the new altar of burnt offerings which they had made. Then all the people fell upon their faces, worshiping and praising the God of heaven. Moreover, Judah and the whole congregation of Israel ordained that the days of the dedication of the altar should be kept in their season from year to year over a period of eight days, from the twenty-fifth day of *Kislev* "with joy and gladness" (1 Maccabees 4:36, 47, 49, 52, 53, 55, 59).

The last verse in this reference bears the word *dedication*, which is *Hanukkah* in the Hebrew and the underlying theme for the holiday. This, then, is the record of the most reliable writing of that period. Since that time a popular saying has arisen: "A great miracle happened there." It is a saying based on a tradition that emerged three centuries later. According to the rabbinical commentary called the *Gemara* (*Shabbat* 21b), only a small amount of holy oil was found when the Maccabees prepared to rekindle the golden *menorah* of the temple. This amount of oil would last only one day, but eight days were needed to prepare additional oil qualified for use in the temple. Nevertheless, by faith they relit the *menorah* and it is said that it remained burning for eight days. The conclusion was that "a great miracle happened there."

Is this actually what happened? Tradition says so. And First Maccabees does tell us that they lit the *menorah*, knowing how long it would take to prepare more oil. So we can only speculate. But the real miracle of *Hanukkah* went far beyond this. The biblical faith of Israel was restored and the temple was rededicated for worship.

There is only one reference in all of Scripture to *Hanukkah*, and it is found in the Gospel of John:

> *"Then came the Feast of Dedication* (Hanukkah) *at Jerusalem. It was winter, and Jesus was in the temple area walking in Solomon's Colonnade" (John 10:22, 23).*

Remember, there is no Old Testament foundation because of the timing of *Hanukkah's* origin. And even in the New Testament we are given no details as to how it was observed. Again we must turn to other sources. Second Maccabees tells us that the first celebration of *Hanukkah* resembled the Feast of Tabernacles (2 Maccabees 10:6, 7). Two centuries later the Jewish historian Flavius Josephus records that in his day *Hanukkah* was being called the Festival of Lights (*Antiquities* XII, 7:7). And the disciples of Hillel and Shammai, who were renowned Jewish sages during Jesus' time, disputed the exact manner of kindling lights for *Hanukkah (Shabbat* 24b). Thus we can discern that in the days of Jesus and the early church, the lighting of lights was a primary feature of the holiday. But beyond that, we cannot be certain how it was observed.

Modern Observance

Today *Hanukkah* is annually celebrated for eight days beginning on the twenty-fifth of *Kislev,* which corresponds to late November or December. The central feature of the celebration, which generally takes place in the home, is the lighting of a special *menorah* that has places for nine candles. Each night for eight nights a new candle is lit. According to custom, on the first night one candle is placed, on the second night two are placed, and so on until the eighth night when the whole candelabra is filled. The daily candles are lit by another candle called the *shammash* (SHAH-mahsh, "the servant"). Special blessings are recited for the lighting of the candles.

Another custom at *Hanukkah* is a game that employs a four-sided top called a *dreidel* (Yiddish for "to turn"). On each of the four sides is the initial Hebrew letter from the words, "A great miracle happened there." The game was popularized by nineteenth-century German Jews. Gift giving has more recently evolved in western countries as a parallel to the Christmas tradition. *Hanukkah* also has its traditional foods, such as *latkes* (LOT-kez, "potato pancakes"), jelly doughnuts and other foods made with oil.

Changes in Observance

The elements of *Hanukkah* observance in today's Jewish homes are, as best as we can conclude, consistent with Jewish observances in the late Second Temple period. The missing element is the temple itself—the object of the "dedication." We might conclude, therefore, that the fulfillment of this holiday took place when the actual temple was standing. The reason for God to intervene and to work a miracle in the days of the Maccabees was to preserve the setting that had been prophesied for the coming of Messiah. For without *Hanukkah*, there would have been no preservation of the culture of Israel. Without the commitment of the Maccabees, there would have been no restoration of biblical worship. Without the dedication of the temple, there would have been no suitable place for Malachi's prophecy to be fulfilled:

> *"'Then suddenly the Lord you are seeking will come to his temple; the messenger of the covenant, whom you desire, will come,' says the Lord Almighty" (Malachi 3:1).*

That is why God raised up the Maccabees. Thanks to the commitment of the Maccabees, God's Word was available and studied, and his program of worship still functioned, so that Messiah might come and reveal their fulfillment. And thanks to the dedication of the temple on the twenty-fifth of *Kislev* in the year 165 B.C., Malachi's words would ring true about two centuries later when Jesus the Messiah appeared in the temple.

Like the *shammash* candle, Jesus was called to be God's consummate servant. His ultimate service to us was his death on our behalf (Matthew 20:28). And like the *shammash,* he brings light to all humanity (John 8:12).

Application

After telling the *Hanukkah* story, review the real miracle of *Hanukkah*.
It is said that "A great miracle happened there." What was that miracle? (Oil lasted eight days.) But what was the most important thing that happened? (The Jewish people were able to live once again according to the Bible and to worship God as he had commanded, not as others wanted them to.)

Discuss the importance of servanthood.
When we think about the Maccabees, we see how they worked to serve the people of Israel. What are some ways that we can be good servants to other people? Like the servant candle that lit the other candles, Jesus the Messiah would also be a servant. "He did not come to be served, but to serve" (Matthew 20:28). The most important service that Jesus did for all people was to bring us salvation. Like the servant candle, Jesus the Messiah brings light to all people. He said these words:

> *"I am the light of the world. Whoever follows me will never walk in darkness, but will have the light of life" (John 8:12).*

We, too, can be lights to the world. What should we tell others about Jesus?

Preparation

Read John 10:22, 23.

Learn the tune to the song "My *Dreidel*." See page 86.

Gather supplies needed for the activities.

❏ Obtain a *Hanukkah menorah* (a nine-branched candlestand) and candles. Or make one, using a simple piece of wood with nine holes (same diameter as the candles) drilled in it. One candle, called the servant, should be higher than the rest. It can be located in the center or on either side. This candle can be elevated by gluing a small piece of wood (with a hole for the candle) on the candlestand.

❏ Obtain or make a *dreidel*, a four-sided top with Hebrew letters on each side.

❏ Obtain *gelt*, foil wrapped chocolate coins (five to ten pieces per child). (Other small pieces of candy or peanuts can be used.)

❏ For the Star of David decoration craft, gather six craft sticks per child, string, marking pens, glitter or sequins, glue or hot glue, instant camera with film. If a camera is unavailable, ask children to bring a picture of themselves to the celebration.

Purchase refreshments. Foods made with oil are traditionally eaten. *Latkes* (potato pancakes) and jelly doughnuts are popular. Or you can make sugar cookies (ideally using *Hanukkah* cookie cutters).

Decide how to present the application of this celebration to contemporary living.

The Celebration

Begin with this introduction.

Hanukkah is a Hebrew word that means 'dedication or setting aside something for a special purpose.' This holiday is celebrated each year for eight nights in late fall or early winter. Each night, candles are lit on a special candlestand called a *menorah*. On the first night one candle is lit, two on the second night, and so on until eight candles are lit on the last night. The daily candles are lit by another candle called the servant candle.

Light the *menorah* and say the blessing.

"Ba-RUKE a-TAH ah-doe-NI el-o-HEY-nu MEL-eck ha-o-LAM ah-SHAIR kid-SHAH-noo bih MITS-vo-tahv vit-zee-VAH-noo, leh had-LEEK nair shell HA-noo-kah."

"Blessed are you, O Lord our God, King of the Universe, who has sanctified us with your commandments, and has commanded us to light the *Hanukkah* candles."

Then take the servant candle and light one or more of the other candles. If you are celebrating during the time of *Hanukkah*, light the number of candles that corresponds to the day of the holiday. Otherwise, you may want to light all of the candles. Light from left to right, ending up at the far right candle.

After lighting the candles, say the following blessing:

"We kindle these lights to commemorate the saving acts and miracles which you performed for our ancestors in those days.

Throughout the eight days of *Hanukkah*, we look at these lights to offer thanks and praise to your great name for your wonders and your salvation. Amen."

Tell the story of *Hanukkah*.

Why do we light these candles? We have to go back in time to find the answer. The history of this holiday goes back to the days between the writing of the Old and New Testaments of the Bible. Israel was under the control of the Syrians, whose leader was Antiochus Epiphanes. He was a man who wanted to get rid of the way people worshiped God in Israel. He forced many changes on the Jewish people and even went so far as to sacrifice a pig on the altar of the temple in Jerusalem. This was not proper according to God's instructions.

So a group of Israelites, who called themselves Maccabees, fought against Antiochus and the Syrians. And after three years, they were able to defeat the Syrian invaders. It then became time to restore the temple for the biblical way of worship. And as they were working in the temple, only a small amount of oil could be found to relight the golden *menorah* of the temple. There was only enough oil to light the lamp for one day, but it would take eight days for the priests to prepare more oil for use in the temple. Yet it is said that the one day's supply of oil glowed in the darkness for all eight days. It was called a miracle.

Today, the lighting of the *menorah* and the other customs of this holiday are reminders of the victory of the Maccabees and the miracle of the lamp burning for eight days. But the most important thing that happened was that the Jewish people were able to live once again according to the Bible and to worship God as he had commanded, not as others wanted them to.

Present the application of this celebration to contemporary living. See page 81.

Make the *Hanukkah* craft.

Make two triangles of craft sticks glued together for each child. Overlay the two triangles into a Star of David and glue together. (See page 62 for an example of this star shape.) Decorate the star with markers, glitter or sequins. Glue a photo of each child to the back of a star so that the picture shows through the center. Loop string through the top of the star and tie into a knot.

Sing "My Dreidel."

A popular custom at *Hanukkah* is a game that uses a four-sided top called a *dreidel*. Before we play this game, we are going to sing a song about it.

I have a little *dreidel*, I made it out of clay.
And when it's dry and ready, then *dreidel* I shall play.
O *dreidel, dreidel, dreidel*, I made it out of clay.
O *dreidel, dreidel, dreidel*; Now *dreidel* I shall play.

Play the *dreidel* game.

Dreidel is a word that means "to turn," just like a top does when it spins. On each of the sides is the first letter from the Hebrew words—*ness gah-DOLE HI-yah shahm*—"A great miracle happened there."

Serve the refreshments.

My Dreidel

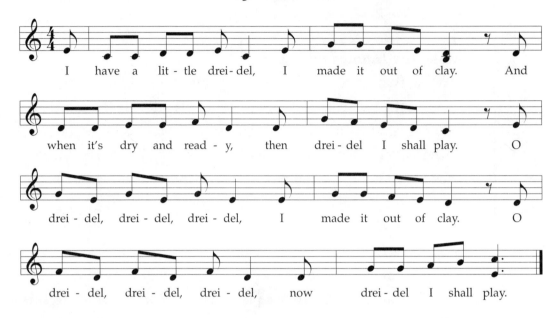

I have a lit - tle drei - del, I made it out of clay. And when it's dry and read - y, then drei - del I shall play. O drei - del, drei - del, drei - del, I made it out of clay. O drei - del, drei - del, drei - del, now drei - del I shall play.

Words by Samuel S. Grossman. Music by Samuel E. Goldfarb, from *The Jewish Home Institute: Chanuko: The Third Week.* (Bureau of Jewish Education, New York.)

Dreidel Game

Dreidel is a word that means "to turn"—
just as a top does when it spins.
On each of the sides is the first letter from the
Hebrew words for "A great miracle happened
there"—*ness gah-DOLE HI-yah shahm.*

Materials for one game
- foil-wrapped chocolate coins (*gelt*)
- a purchased *dreidel* or homemade *dreidel* cube

Name of Letter	Sound	Result
noon	**N**	Do nothing
GIM-mel	**G**	Take all
heh	**H**	Take half
shin	**SH**	Add one to the pile

Each player starts out with an equal number of *gelt* (foil-wrapped chocolate coins), candy or peanuts. Before starting, each player puts one piece into the pile.

Players take turns spinning the *dreidel* and doing what the letter on top indicates.

Each time the pile is emptied, all players add one piece and play continues.

The game is over when one player has all the pieces or when a time limit has been reached.

Dreidel

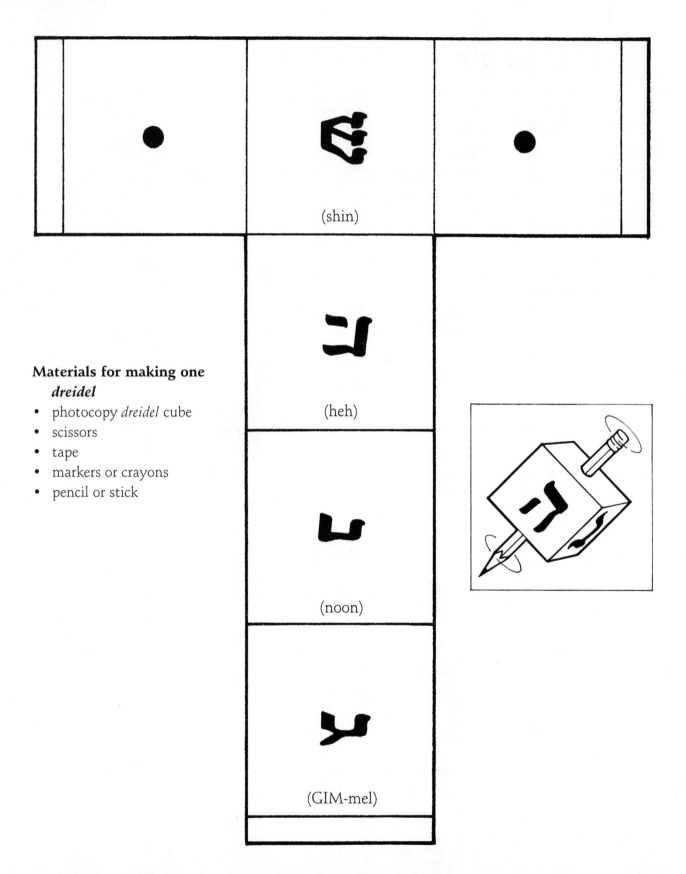

(shin)

(heh)

(noon)

(GIM-mel)

Materials for making one *dreidel*

- photocopy *dreidel* cube
- scissors
- tape
- markers or crayons
- pencil or stick

HANUKKAH

The Festival of Lights

_____

Date

_____

Time

_____

Place

The Feast

of

Esther

Purim (Lots)

BIBLICAL MONTH	*Adar*
MODERN EQUIVALENT	February/March
O.T. REFERENCE	Esther 9:23-32

An Overview

The correct pronunciation of *Purim* is poo-REEM, but it is commonly accented POO-rim (never "pure-im"). This holiday is traditionally celebrated early in the springtime. It is based on the book of Esther and tells the story of what took place among the Jewish people who remained in Persia after the Babylonian captivity ended. This celebration has three parts: Children can begin by making noisemakers called *groggers* (GRAH-gers) and masks for the characters of the story to follow. Then the scroll of Esther is read by the leader and participants (with portions divided into actual roles). Guidelines are provided for more ambitious leaders who want to adapt the text for a drama or puppet show. Finally, everyone enjoys a traditional holiday pastry known as *hamantaschen* (HAH-mahn-tah-shen). Everyone learns about God's protection of the Jewish people and about how one person can make a difference in his or her world.

Biblical Heritage

After serving seventy years of captivity in Babylon, many Jews returned to Jerusalem in 536 B.C. to rebuild the temple. Others stayed behind—some who would later return with Ezra in 457 B.C., some who went with Nehemiah to rebuild the walls of the city in 444 B.C., and some who never left. The book of Esther tells a story about the Jewish people who were still there after the return of the first exiles (c. 478-473 B.C.).

Babylon had been conquered by Persia. Their king at the time of this story is known in the Hebrew as Ahasuerus (ah-has-oo-er-os) and in the Greek as Xerxes (ZERKS-ees). He was a ruler known for his vacillation and susceptibility to the manipulation of others. One of his ambitious ministers, Haman (HAY-mun), plotted to annihilate the Jewish people living in the empire and persuaded the king to agree to his plan. But thanks to the efforts of two Jewish people, a man named Mordecai (MORE-de-kai) and his relative named Esther who had become queen of Persia, the plot was thwarted and the Jews were spared. In the end the Jewish people were given the right to defend themselves and overcame those who sought to destroy them.

The name *Purim* is a plural Hebrew word meaning "lots." The name is taken from the lots that were used by Haman to ascertain the date for the destruction of the Jews, a common practice among cultures of the ancient near east for determining divine will. In commemoration of this day that was slated for defeat but became a victory, Mordecai and Esther decreed that all Jews and "all who join with them" should celebrate *Purim* on an annual basis (Esther 9:27-32).

Historical Observance

The original instructions for the celebration of this holiday are limited. It was simply to be a time of "feasting and joy and giving presents" (Esther 9:22). Since *Purim* was instituted at the end of the writing of the Old Testament and there are no references in the New Testament, our only other sources of description are the ancient historical books. The principal characteristic seems to be that of a carnival, marked by masquerade and merriment. Because its revelry easily became excessive, Jewish leaders in Jerusalem expressed some concern on importing this holiday from Persia, but in time its observance became accepted throughout Jewish society *(Megillah 7a; Y. Megillah I)*.

Modern Observance

In synagogues today, the celebration of *Purim* centers around the reading of Esther from a special scroll called a *megillah* (meh-GILL-ah). Unlike *Torah* scrolls that utilize two wooden rollers, a *megillah* uses only one. The reading is highly interactive, with the audience booing and ridiculing the villain Haman along with using *grogger* noisemakers whenever his name is mentioned. Children especially come in costume, though in Israel the carnival atmosphere carries over into every part of society.

One of the traditional foods eaten at this time is *hamantaschen,* a pastry originally made with poppyseed pockets. Today it is made with a variety of fillings. The popular belief is that this pastry is associated with Haman in some manner. It has been claimed that the triangular shape comes from the type of hat worn by Haman. This legend is suspect since this style of hat was popular in eighteenth and nineteenth century Europe, not in ancient Persia where the round turban was the norm. Another explanation that the shape resembles the ears of Haman is equally untenable because pointed ears were considered to be signs of evil and would not have been something a person would eat. It is more likely that Jewish bakers prepared poppyseed pockets (Yiddish, *muntaschen)* as a play on words, renamed them *hamentaschen,* and a delicious tradition was born.

Changes in Observance

One of the peculiarities of Esther is that the name of God is never mentioned in this book. That fact has caused some critics to discount its authenticity and rightful place in the biblical canon. Yet God's providential care for Israel is present as his hand moved the hearts of the people in the story. Many times individuals and nations have set out to destroy the Jewish people, and while they have been chastened and persecuted, God has always intervened and preserved them. The Scriptures declare

"He that watches over Israel will neither slumber nor sleep" (Psalm 121:4).

And again in the context of the very prophecy of the New Covenant—a covenant which was fulfilled in the death and resurrection of Jesus the Messiah—we have this promise regarding the Jewish people

"This is what the Lord says, he who appoints the sun to shine by day, who decrees the moon and stars to shine by night, who stirs up the sea so that its waves roar—the Lord Almighty is his name: 'Only if these decrees vanish from my sight,' declares the Lord, 'will the descendants of Israel ever cease to be a nation before me'" (Jeremiah 31:35, 36).

The story of *Purim* is an illustration that God intends to sustain the Jewish people throughout every generation. And he works through individuals, sometimes with just one or two at a time as demonstrated in the book of Esther, to accomplish his plans. But beyond their physical preservation, the Scriptures make it clear that he desires their spiritual redemption as well. His message is distinct: "Return, O Israel, to the Lord your God" (Hosea 14:1). And the way of return is through Jesus the Messiah (John 14:6). Thus the holiday of *Purim*, as in the case of all other biblical holidays, foreshadows God's greater program of redemption and finds its ultimate fulfillment in the Messiah.

Note: The holiday of *Purim* is not specifically mentioned in the New Testament.

Application

At the end of the reading of the story from the book of Esther, discuss some of the points raised by this story.

How might hatred take control of us? Did it do Haman any good to be so hateful? Should we ever hate anyone? Jesus said

"You have heard that it was said, Love your neighbor and hate your enemy. But I tell you: Love your enemies and pray for those who persecute you" (Matthew 5:43, 44).

Examine the actions of Esther and discuss how she made a difference in her world.

Why was Esther afraid to go before the king? (She might die if she went to the king on her own.) Even though she was afraid, did she still do what she had to do?

John the Apostle wrote

There is no fear in love. But perfect love drives out fear, because fear has to do with punishment. The one who fears is not made perfect in love. We love because he first loved us. If anyone says, "I love God," yet hates his brother, he is a liar. For anyone who does not love his brother, whom he has seen, cannot love God, whom he has not seen (1 John 4:18-20).

Esther was just one person, but she made a difference in her world. The Bible teaches that one person, Adam, brought sin into the world and one person, Jesus, completed salvation for the world

For just as through the disobedience of the one man the many were made sinners, so also through the obedience of the one man the many will be made righteous (Romans 5:19).

Can you think of a way that you can make a difference in the places where you go or where you live?

Preparation

Read the book of Esther.

Encourage the wearing of costumes. *Purim* is a festive holiday in which children often wear costumes. They can be encouraged to dress like kings and queens.

Gather supplies needed for crafts.

Groggers
- ❑ paper plates
- ❑ tongue depressors
- ❑ dry beans
- ❑ marking pens
- ❑ stapler
- ❑ glue

Masks
- ❑ paper plates
- ❑ yarn
- ❑ construction paper
- ❑ marking pens
- ❑ glitter
- ❑ scissors
- ❑ stapler
- ❑ glue

Bake the traditional *hamantaschen* pastry. See page 105.

Decide how to present the application of this celebration to contemporary living.

The Celebration

Begin with this introduction.

The holiday of *Purim* is celebrated each year early in the spring-time. It is based on the book of Esther and tells the story of what took place among the Jewish people who remained in Persia after the Babylonian captivity ended. Traditionally, the central event of the holiday is the reading of a special scroll called a *megillah* (meh-GILL-ah). That means the words were written on a large piece of parchment, like paper, and then rolled around a piece of wood. Other scrolls of the Bible were put on two rollers, but a *megillah* has only one.

The word *purim* means "lots" because Haman, the evil character of the story, cast lots to determine the date when the Jewish people would be destroyed. Whenever the name of Haman is mentioned it is customary to boo and to sound noisemakers called *groggers*.

Make the crafts.

• Grogger

Fold a paper plate in half. Fill with beans and staple closed. Glue or staple tongue depressor to the end. Decorate the plate.

• Masks

Staple yarn on both sides of plate (to tie on head). Cut out holes for eyes and mouth. Decorate the plate, making the face look like the king, Queen Esther, Mordecai, Haman, or the king's advisor.

Choose a format for telling the story from the book of Esther. See ideas on page 97.

Option 1: Readers Theater

Make sufficient photocopies of the story of Esther (pages 98—104) for all participants or six copies for only those doing the reading.

The story has been condensed and divided into the following roles:

Leader	King
Esther	Mordecai
Haman	Advisor

An adult normally reads the Leader part, although these sections can also be divided up among children if you desire.

Option 2: Drama

This is similar to option one but also includes participants moving about on a "stage." They would enter and exit as needed and basically follow the cues of the text. They would not need to memorize the lines. They could hold the "script" and read their parts.

As a variation to this option, some adults or older children could present the drama for everyone else.

Option 3: Puppet Show

The participants read their roles using puppets that you make or have on hand. A stage can be made out of a large cardboard box or PVC pipe and cloth. Again, like the drama option, adults or older children could present the puppet show for everyone else.

Read the story.

Whenever the name of Haman is mentioned everyone can momentarily boo and sound their *groggers*.

The Narrative From the Book of Esther

Leader

This is what happened during the time of King Ahasuerus (Ah-has-oo-er-os) who reigned from his royal throne in the citadel of Susa, the fortress capital of Persia. In the third year of his reign, he gave a banquet lasting seven days for all the people from the least to the greatest. On the seventh day, the king commanded queen Vashti (VASH-tee) to come before him to show her beauty to the people and nobles. When queen Vashti refused to come, the king became angry. He talked to his experts in law and justice.

King

According to law, what must be done to queen Vashti? She has not obeyed the command of the king.

Advisor

Queen Vashti has done wrong, not only against the king but also against all the nobles and all the people of the king. Everyone will say . . .

Everyone

The King commanded the queen to appear before him, but she would not.

Advisor

So, let a royal order be written that cannot be changed. It should say that the queen is never again to enter the presence of the king. Also let the king give her royal position to someone better than she.

Leader

The king was pleased with this advice. So he sent orders to all parts of the kingdom, proclaiming in the language of all the people that every man should be ruler over his own household. Later the king remembered Vashti and what she had done. Then the king's personal attendants said . . .

Advisor

Let a search be made for beautiful young women for the king. Then let the girl who pleases the king be made queen instead of Vashti.

Leader

The king liked this advice and he followed it. Many girls were brought to the harem, the place where the king's women lived. Now there was in the citadel of Susa a Jewish man named Mordecai (MORE-de-kai). Many years before, he had been taken from Jerusalem and put into slavery in Babylon. Mordecai had a cousin named Esther whom he had adopted as his own daughter when her father and mother died. When she was brought to the harem, Esther did not reveal that she was an Israelite just as Mordecai had instructed her. When Esther's turn came to go before the king, he liked Esther more than any of the other women so he chose her.

King

From this day on, Esther will be queen instead of Vashti. Place a royal crown upon her head and on this day there will be a holiday throughout all the provinces.

Leader

During this time, Mordecai walked back and forth every day near the courtyard. One day as Mordecai was sitting at the king's gate, two of the king's officers became angry and planned to kill King Ahasuerus. Mordecai overheard the plot and told

queen Esther who reported it to the king.

Esther

O King, there is an evil plot by two of your officers. It was discovered by a good and honorable man named Mordecai.

King

Very well. My nobles will investigate this report, and if it is true, these two officials will be hanged on a gallows.

Leader

After these events, King Ahasuerus honored a man named Haman (HAY-man) and gave him a place of honor higher than all other nobles. Everyone bowed down and revered Haman. But Mordecai would not bow down or give him reverence. Then the royal officials at the king's gate asked Mordecai . . .

Advisor

Why do you disobey the king's command?

Mordecai

Because of my faith, I cannot bow down to any thing or any person.

Leader

Day after day they spoke to him but Mordecai refused to agree. When Haman saw that Mordecai would not bow down, he became very angry. And when he learned who Mordecai's people were, he looked for a way to destroy not only Mordecai but all of the Jewish people in the kingdom. In order to choose a day for their destruction, they cast the *pur,* meaning the "lot," which is an object used to decide something by chance. The lot fell on the twelfth month, the month of *Adar* (Ah-DAR). Then Haman said to the King . . .

Haman

There is a certain people, called Jews, scattered among the provinces of your kingdom who keep themselves separate. Their customs are different from those of all other people, and they do not obey the king's laws. We should not accept them. If it pleases the king, let an order be given to destroy them.

King

Very well, Haman. Do whatever you want to those people.

Leader

The royal secretaries came and orders were sent to all the king's provinces to destroy all the Jews—young and old, women and little children—on a single day, the thirteenth day of the month of *Adar.* In every province to which the order of the king came, there was great sadness among the Jews. When Mordecai learned of all that had been done, he tore his clothes, put on sackcloth and ashes, and went out into the city, crying bitterly.

When Esther's maids came and told her about Mordecai, she was very upset. Then Esther sent an attendant to speak to Mordecai in the open square of the city in front of the king's gate.

Mordecai

A terrible thing is about to happen. Go back and tell Esther to go to the king to beg for mercy and plead with him for her people.

Leader

The attendant went back and reported to Esther what Mordecai had said. Then she instructed him to say to Mordecai . . .

Esther

All people of the kingdom know that anyone who goes to the king in the inner court without being asked will be put to death. What can I do?

Leader

When Esther's words were reported to Mordecai, he sent back this answer . . .

Mordecai

Do not think that since you live in the king's house you will escape. For if you remain completely silent at this time, then deliverance for the Jewish people will come from another place, but you will perish. For who knows if you have come to the kingdom for such a time as this?

Esther

I will not eat for three days. When this is done, I will go to the king, even though it is against the law. And if I perish, I perish.

Leader

On the third day Esther put on her royal robes and stood in the inner court of the palace. The king was sitting on his royal throne in the hall, facing the entrance. When he saw

queen Esther standing in the court, he held out to her the gold scepter that was in his hand. So Esther approached and touched the tip of the scepter.

King

What is it, Queen Esther? What is your request? Even up to half the kingdom, it will be given to you.

Esther

If it pleases the king, let the king, together with Haman, come today to a banquet I have prepared for you.

King

Bring Haman at once so that we may do what Esther asks.

Leader

So the king and Haman went to the banquet Esther had prepared. And the king asked Esther . . .

King

Now what is your petition? It will be given to you.

Esther

If the king regards me with favor, let the king and Haman come tomorrow to another banquet that I will prepare. Then I will answer the king's question.

Leader

Haman went out that day in a happy mood. But when he saw that Mordecai at the king's gate still did not honor him, he became angry with Mordecai. Later, at his home, Haman told his wife and friends about all the ways the king had honored him.

Haman

I'm the only person queen Esther invited to join the king at her banquet tomorrow. But all this gives me no happiness as long as I see that man, Mordecai, sitting at the king's gate.

Leader

His wife, Zeresh (ZEHR-esh), recommended that he build a gallows and ask the king to have Mordecai hanged on it. Haman liked this idea, so he had the gallows built. Later that night the king could not sleep; so he ordered the book of the chronicles, the record of his reign, to be read to him. There in the book was the record of the time when

Mordecai discovered the two officers who had planned to kill King Ahasuerus.

King

What honor and recognition has Mordecai received for this?

Advisor

Nothing has been done for him.

King

I see. Look, here comes Haman. I shall ask him. Haman, what do you think should be done for the man the king wants to honor?

Haman

Who would the king want to honor more than me? I know; have servants bring a royal robe and a horse with a royal crest on its head. Let them put the robe on the man whom the king wants to honor and lead him on the horse through the city streets, proclaiming, "This is what is done for the man the king delights to honor!"

King

Very well, Haman. Get the robe and the horse and do just as you have suggested. And do it for Mordecai, the Jewish man, who sits at the king's gate.

Leader

Haman was shocked because he thought the king was going to honor him. But he put the robe on Mordecai and led him on horseback through the city streets, proclaiming before him . . .

Haman

This is what is done for the man the king wants to honor!

This is what is done for the man the king wants to honor!

Leader

Afterward, Haman rushed home with his head covered in grief, but he was soon summoned to the banquet of queen Esther. During the banquet the king again asked . . .

King

Queen Esther, what is your request? I will give you up to half the kingdom.

Esther

If I have found favor with you, O king, and if it pleases your majesty, grant me my life and spare my people. For there is a plan to destroy them.

King

Who is the man who has dared to do such a thing?

Esther

The enemy is this terrible Haman.

Leader

The king got up and went out into the palace garden. But Haman, realizing that the king was deciding what to do with him, stayed behind to beg Esther for his life. Just as the king returned from the palace garden to the banquet hall, Haman was falling on the couch where Esther was resting.

King

Will he even harm the queen while she is with me in the house?

Leader

As soon as the word left the king's mouth, they covered Haman's face. So they hanged Haman on the gallows he had prepared for Mordecai. And when Esther told how she was related to Mordecai, he was brought into the presence of the king. The king took off his signet ring, and presented it to Mordecai. Esther again pleaded with the king about the evil plan of Haman against the Jewish people . . .

Esther

If it pleases the king, let an order be written overruling the one that Haman gave to destroy the Jews in all the king's provinces. For how can I bear to see disaster fall on my people?

King

No order written in the king's name and sealed with his ring can be changed. But another order can be written in the king's name for the Jewish people.

Mordecai

This order shall give the Jewish people in every city the right to protect themselves.

Leader

In every province, wherever the order went, there was much celebrating.

And many people of other nationalities became Jews in that day. On the thirteenth day of the month of *Adar*, the original order was to be carried out. On this day when the enemies of the Jews had hoped to overpower them, the Jewish people fought back and defeated their enemies. On the next day they rested.

Mordecai

Let everyone celebrate these days as the time when the Jewish people got relief from their enemies, when their sorrow was turned into joy and their sadness into celebration.

Leader

Because of everything that happened, the Jews established a holiday celebration every year as a custom for themselves and their descendants and anyone else who joins them. These days called *Purim,* meaning lots, should be remembered in every generation by every family and in every city.

Present the application of this celebration to contemporary living. See page 94.

Enjoy *hamantaschen* pastry.

Hamentaschen Pastry

Ingredients

1/4 lb. cream cheese	**Filling**
1/4 lb. margarine	raspberry jam
2 1/2 cups flour	raisins
2 teaspoons baking powder	nuts
1/2 cup sugar	1/2 tablespoon lemon juice
2 eggs	1/2 tablespoon cinnamon
3 tablespoons sour cream	
juice and grated rind of 1 lemon	

Dough: Cream together butter and cream cheese. Add eggs and sugar. Beat until smooth. Add sour cream and lemon. Gradually add flour and baking powder. Refrigerate three to four hours or overnight. Roll out dough to 1/8 inch thickness and cut into circles.

Filling: Heat jam. Add enough raisins and nuts to make a thick mixture. Add 1/2 tablespoon lemon and cinnamon.

Put one teaspoon filling in the middle of each dough circle. Pinch up three sides into a triangular shape, leaving some filling showing on top. If the dough does not hold when you pinch the sides, wet the inner edge with water first. Brush with egg whites if you desire. Bake at 375 degrees until light brown. Makes 35 to 45.

Grogger

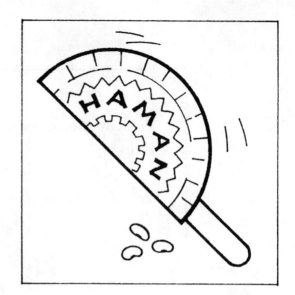

Materials to make one *grogger*

- paper plate
- tongue depressor
- beans
- stapler
- glue or tape
- photocopies of page 109

1. Fold a paper plate in half.
2. Fill with beans and staple closed.
3. Glue or staple a tongue depressor to the end.
4. Decorate the plate or color the pattern (page 109) and glue it to the plate.

Masks

Materials for one mask

- photocopy of page 109
- paper plate
- scissors
- crayons or markers
- glue
- tongue depressor
- Option: yarn for hair

1. Cut items from page 109.
2. Glue onto paper plates.
3. Glue or staple the tongue depressor to the plate to make a hand-held mask.
4. Option: Draw and color your own mask.

THE FEAST of ESTHER
A FESTIVAL of LOTS

PURIM

You are invited to
a celebration of

PURIM

Date
_____

Time
_____

Place
_____

Scripture Index

Genesis
22:1-19	43

Exodus
12	11
12:14, 15	8
13:21	66
19:1-25	28
23:14-17	67

Leviticus
6:17	8
16:1-34	54, 57
17:11	54, 55
20:7	54
23:1-44	4, 28
23:5-8	8, 11
23:11	28
23:15-21	29
23:14-17	30, 67
23:23-35	42
23:26-28	57
23:29	55
23:33-44	66, 70

Numbers
9:17	66
29:1-6	42
33:3	10

Deuteronomy
16:6	10

Ruth
1—4	31
1:16	33

Esther
9:22	93
9:27-32	92

Psalms
32:1	54
103:12	56
113—118	9
118:25	67
121:4	93

Isaiah
9:6, 7	68
53	9

Jeremiah
31:33	30
31:35, 36	94

Ezekiel
18:20	54
36:26	30

Hosea
7:4	8

Malachi
3:1	81

Matthew
5:43, 44	94
9:37, 38	31
20:28	81
26:19	10
27:45	10

John
7:2—9:5	65
7:37, 38	68
8:12	81
9:5	68
10:22, 23	80
10:27	44
14:2, 3	69
14:6	94
14:26	31

Acts
2:1-47	30, 35

Romans
4:7	56
5:8	44
5:19	94
6:23	54

1 Corinthians
5:7	10
15:20	29

2 Corinthians
5:1, 4	68

1 Thessalonians
4:16	44

2 Timothy
3:16	30

Hebrews
7:27	56
9:11—10:22	56
11:28	10

James
2:10	34

1 John
4:18-20	94

Pronunciation Guide

afikomen 9	ah-fee-KO-men	*Maccabees* 78	MAC-ah-bees
Ahasuerus 92	ah-has-oo-er-os	*maror* 21	mah-ROAR
		matzah 8	MAHT-sah
chometz 9	hah-METS	*matzot* 11	maht-ZOAT
		megillah 93	meh-GILL-ah
Dayeinu 8	dah-YEH-noo	*menorah* 78	men-NO-rah
dreidel 78	DRAY-del	*Mordecai* 92	MORE-de-kai
etrog 66	EH-trog	*omer* 28	OH-mare
groggers 92	GRAH-gers	*Purim* 92	poo-reem
haggadah 8	hah-gah-DAH (huh-GAH-dah)	*Rosh Hashanah* 42	rosh ha-SHAH-nah
hallah 61	HALL-ah		
Hallel 9	ha-LELL	*seder* 8	SAY-der
hamantaschen 92		*shammash* 80	SHAH-mahsh
	HAH-mahn-tah-shen	*Shavuot* 28	SHAH-voo-oat
Hanukkah 78	HA-noo-kah	*shofar* 42	SHO-far
haroset 21	hah-RO-set	*shofarim* 46	sho-far-EEM
Hoshana Rabba 67		*Simhat Torah* 67	SIM-hot TOE-rah
	ho-SHAH-nah RAH-bah	*sukkah* 66	SOO-kah
		Sukkot 66	soo-COAT
kippah 54	KIP-pah	*tashlich* 43	tash-LEEK
Kol Nidre 55	cole NEE-dray	*Torah* 28	TOE-rah
lulav 66	LOO-lahv	*yarmulke* 59	YAR-mul-kah
		Yom Kippur 54	yoam kip-POOR

Note: Page number refers to the first use of a Hebrew or Yiddish term.

Additional Resources

The Gospel in the Feasts of Israel, by Victor Buksbazen, West Collingswood, New Jersey: The Friends of Israel, 1954.

The Passover Anthology, by Philip Goodman, Philadelphia: The Jewish Publication Society of America, 1993.

The Jewish Book of Why, by Alfred J. Kolatch, Middle Village, New York: Jonathan David Publishers, 1981,

The Book of Jewish Customs, by Harvey Lutske, Northvale, New Jersey: Jason Aronson Inc., 1995.

The Everlasting Tradition, by Galen Peterson, Grand Rapids, Mich.: Kregel Publications, 1995.

Celebrate the Feasts, by Martha Zimmerman, Minneapolis, Minn.: Bethany House Publishers, 1981.

The Jewish Publication Society offers *The Kid's Catalog of Jewish Holidays,* compiled by David Adler.

Other references used in preparing this guide:

Messianic Services for the Festivals and Holy Days, by John Fischer, Palm Harbor, Florida: Menorah Ministries, 1992.

The Jewish Festivals, by Hayim Schauss, New York: Schocken Books, 1938.

Tabernacle Shadows of the Better Sacrifices, East Rutherford, New Jersey: Dawn Publications, 1881.

The New Covenant Passover Haggadah, Pleasant Hill, Calif.: American Remnant Mission, 1989.